A GLOBAL BATTLEGROUND: THE FIGHT AGAINST ISLAMIST EXTREMISM AT HOME AND ABROAD

HEARING

BEFORE THE

COMMITTEE ON HOMELAND SECURITY

HOUSE OF REPRESENTATIVES

ONE HUNDRED FOURTEENTH CONGRESS

FIRST SESSION

MARCH 24, 2015

Serial No. 114–11

Printed for the use of the Committee on Homeland Security

Available via the World Wide Web: http://www.gpo.gov/fdsys/

U.S. GOVERNMENT PUBLISHING OFFICE

94–886 PDF   WASHINGTON : 2015

For sale by the Superintendent of Documents, U.S. Government Publishing Office
Internet: bookstore.gpo.gov   Phone: toll free (866) 512–1800; DC area (202) 512–1800
Fax: (202) 512–2104   Mail: Stop IDCC, Washington, DC 20402–0001

COMMITTEE ON HOMELAND SECURITY

MICHAEL T. MCCAUL, Texas, *Chairman*

LAMAR SMITH, Texas
PETER T. KING, New York
MIKE ROGERS, Alabama
CANDICE S. MILLER, Michigan, *Vice Chair*
JEFF DUNCAN, South Carolina
TOM MARINO, Pennsylvania
LOU BARLETTA, Pennsylvania
SCOTT PERRY, Pennsylvania
CURT CLAWSON, Florida
JOHN KATKO, New York
WILL HURD, Texas
EARL L. "BUDDY" CARTER, Georgia
MARK WALKER, North Carolina
BARRY LOUDERMILK, Georgia
MARTHA MCSALLY, Arizona
JOHN RATCLIFFE, Texas
VACANCY

BENNIE G. THOMPSON, Mississippi
LORETTA SANCHEZ, California
SHEILA JACKSON LEE, Texas
JAMES R. LANGEVIN, Rhode Island
BRIAN HIGGINS, New York
CEDRIC L. RICHMOND, Louisiana
WILLIAM R. KEATING, Massachusetts
DONALD M. PAYNE, JR., New Jersey
FILEMON VELA, Texas
BONNIE WATSON COLEMAN, New Jersey
KATHLEEN M. RICE, New York
NORMA J. TORRES, California

BRENDAN P. SHIELDS, *Staff Director*
JOAN V. O'HARA, *General Counsel*
MICHAEL S. TWINCHEK, *Chief Clerk*
I. LANIER AVANT, *Minority Staff Director*

CONTENTS

_____

A GLOBAL BATTLEGROUND: THE FIGHT AGAINST ISLAMIST EXTREMISM AT HOME AND ABROAD

Tuesday, March 24, 2015

U.S. HOUSE OF REPRESENTATIVES,
COMMITTEE ON HOMELAND SECURITY,
Washington, DC.

The committee met, pursuant to call, at 10:38 a.m., in Room 311, Cannon House Office Building, Hon. Michael T. McCaul [Chairman of the committee] presiding.

Present: Representatives McCaul, Smith, King, Perry, Katko, Hurd, Carter, Walker, Loudermilk, McSally, Ratcliffe, Thompson, Jackson Lee, Higgins, Richmond, Keating, Vela, Watson Coleman, and Rice.

Chairman MCCAUL. The Committee on Homeland Security will come to order.

Before we start, I would like to take a moment of silence out of respect for the 150 victims of the German airline crash today in the French Alps.

We send our deepest condolences to their families and to our allies as they deal with this tragedy.

I now recognize myself for an opening statement.

The committee is meeting today to hear testimony on the global war against Islamist terror. Before 9/11 we failed to recognize this threat when it was right before our eyes. This failure brought us into war with violent Islamist extremism, the perversion of a religion into a deeply insidious worldview. Any attempt to deny the ideological underpinnings of the threat endangers our security.

Throughout history we have seen power vacuums filled by violent groups, deranged dictators, and extremist ideologies. Nowhere is this more evident than with the rise of Islamist terror groups, which have spread like wildfire on this President's watch because of two glaring leadership failures.

The first failure was the President's decision to spin a false narrative. The White House proclaimed our fight was against core al-Qaeda and that that group was on the path to defeat. In reality, the Jihadist threat had metastasized. The President refused to characterize the Fort Hood and Boston Marathon attacks for what they were—acts of brutal Islamist terrorism.

The second leadership failure was the President's decision to dismantle America's counterterrorism policies and return to a pre-9/11 law enforcement posture. The President tried to close Guantanamo Bay and release hardened terrorists, sought to give terrorists the same legal protections as U.S. citizens, negotiated and swapped hostages with terrorists, and failed to prevent the rise of ISIS and the emergence of al-Qaeda sanctuaries.

A year after the President called ISIS the JV team, the organization could draw on over 20,000 foreign fighters and has been linked to 29 terrorist plots or attacks targeting the West. What I thought was interesting: The day the President said the global war on terror was effectively over was the day that al-Baghdadi created ISIS.

ISIS now controls territory the size of Belgium, governs millions of people, draws on billions of dollars in revenue, and commands tens of thousands of foot-soldiers. Terrorist safe havens have spread across the Middle East and Northern Africa. Last week, ISIS claimed responsibility for the terror attack in the museum in Tunisia. The gunmen involved had received training in Libyan terror camps.

ISIS also claimed responsibility for the horrific attacks on mosques in Yemen, which killed more than 150 people. Yemen's instability has led to the evacuation of our remaining forces and will further empower extremists. This situation is alarming, given that al-Qaeda's premier bomb-makers in AQAP have been targeting the homeland and Western interests for years.

Over the past year, Islamist terrorists have struck Western cities, including Paris, Sydney, Ottawa, Copenhagen, and Brussels. We have witnessed the reach of extremists here at home, as well. An Ohio-based ISIS sympathizer was arrested in January for plotting to attack the United States Capitol.

Last week, an ISIS-aligned hacking group posted the names, photos, and addresses of 100 American service members, calling their brothers residing in America to attack these individuals.

At the other end of the Islamist extremist spectrum we face Iran, the world's leading state sponsor of terrorism, responsible for killing Americans for more than 3 decades.

In 2011 it attempted to assassinate the Saudi Arabian ambassador in what would have been a mass-casualty attack here in Washington.

The Iranian regime is on the march, destabilizing the Middle East and stoking sectarian conflict. Yet this administration has given up on rolling back Iran's nuclear threat, and it continually fails to recognize the regime as part of the radical Islamist threat. As Prime Minister Netanyahu said before this Congress, ''Iran and ISIS are competing for the crown of militant Islam.''

We continue to face dual threats here at home, foreign fighters and home-grown terrorism. More than 180 Americans have tried or succeeded in joining extremists in Syria and Iraq, along with 3,000 to 5,000 other Westerners with visa-free access to the United States. Armed with military training and terrorist connections, these individuals are only a plane flight away.

Islamist radicals are also tailoring their hateful ideology toward Western audiences on social media and recruiting home-grown fanatics. The easy transmission of extremist propaganda on the internet has elevated the threat to the homeland. For example, there have been at least 97 home-grown terror plots or attacks in the United States since 9/11, and more than three-fourths of them have taken place in the past 5 years.

The rise of radicalism we are witnessing today is not just a passing phenomenon. The war against Islamist terror will be the great struggle of our lifetime, the great struggle of this century, and I believe we have a moral and strategic obligation to fight it with all tools at our disposal.

Just as Communism and fascism before it, Islamic extremism is a cancer that must be destroyed. To blunt their progress we can begin by coalescing around a comprehensive strategy to wipe out these Jihadists and their twisted ideologies.

Our purposes should be clear. It must be the policy of the United States to confront and defeat Islamist terror groups wherever they are, and prevent their reemergence in order to ensure the long-term security of the United States and our allies.

I look forward to hearing from the distinguished witnesses we have here today, including the former Speaker of the House, Mr. Gingrich.

[The statement of Chairman McCaul follows:]

STATEMENT OF CHAIRMAN MICHAEL T. MCCAUL

MARCH 24, 2015

Before 9/11, we failed to recognize the threat when it was right before our eyes. This failure brought us into war with violent Islamist extremism—the perversion of a religion into a deeply insidious worldview. Any attempt to deny the ideological underpinnings of the threat endangers our security.

Throughout history, we have seen power vacuums filled by violent groups, deranged dictators, and extremist ideologies. Nowhere is this more evident than with the rise of Islamist terror groups, which have spread like wildfire on this President's watch because of two glaring leadership failures.

The first failure was the President's decision to spin a false narrative. The White House proclaimed our fight was against "core" al-Qaeda and that the group was "on the path to defeat." In reality, the jihadist threat had metastasized. The President refused to characterize the Ft. Hood and Boston Marathon attacks for what they were—acts of brutal Islamist terrorism.

The second leadership failure was the President's decision to dismantle America's counterterrorism policies and return to a pre-9/11 law-enforcement posture. The President tried to close Guantanamo Bay and release hardened terrorists; sought to give terrorists the same legal protections as U.S. citizens; negotiated and swapped hostages with terrorists; and failed to prevent the rise of ISIS and the emergence of al-Qaeda sanctuaries.

A year after the President called ISIS the "JV team," the organization can draw on over 20,000 foreign fighters and has been linked to 29 terrorist plots or attacks targeting the West. And the day the President said the global war on terror was effectively over was the day al Baghdadi created ISIS. ISIS now controls territory the size of Belgium, governs millions of people, draws on billions of dollars in revenue, and commands tens of thousands of foot soldiers.

Terrorist safe havens have spread across the Middle East and North Africa. Last week, ISIS claimed responsibility for the terror attack in a museum in Tunisia; the gunmen involved had received training in Libyan terror camps. ISIS also claimed responsibility for the horrific attacks on mosques in Yemen which killed more than 150 people. Yemen's instability has led to the evacuation of our remaining forces and will further empower extremists. This situation is alarming given that al-Qaeda's premier bomb-makers in AQAP have been targeting the homeland and Western interests for years.

Over the past year, Islamist terrorists have struck Western cities, including Paris, Sydney, Ottawa, Copenhagen, and Brussels. We have witnessed the reach of extremists here at home as well. An Ohio-based ISIS sympathizer was arrested in January for plotting to attack the U.S. Capitol. Last week, an ISIS-aligned hacking group posted the names, photos, and addresses of 100 American service members, calling their "brothers residing in America" to attack these individuals.

At the other end of the Islamist extremist spectrum, we face Iran, the world's leading state sponsor of terrorism responsible for killing Americans for more than three decades. In 2011, it attempted to assassinate the Saudi Arabian ambassador in what would have been a mass-casualty attack here in Washington.

The Iranian regime is on the march, destabilizing the Middle East and stoking sectarian conflict. Yet this administration has given up on rolling back Iran's nuclear threat and it continually fails to recognize the regime as part of the radical Islamist threat. As Israeli Prime Minister Netanyahu said before Congress, ''Iran and ISIS are competing for the crown of militant Islam.''

We continue to face ''dual threats'' here at home: Foreign fighters and home-grown terrorism. More than 180 Americans have tried or succeeded in joining extremists in Syria and Iraq along with 3,000–5,000 other Westerners with visa-free access to the United States. Armed with military training and terrorist connections, these individuals are only a plane flight away.

Islamist radicals are also tailoring their hateful ideology toward Western audiences on social media and recruiting home-grown fanatics. The easy transmission of extremist propaganda on the internet has elevated the threat to the homeland. For example, there have been at least 97 home-grown terror plots or attacks in the United States since 9/11—and more than three-fourths of them have taken place in the past 5 years.

The rise of radicalism we are witnessing today is not just a passing phenomenon. The War against Islamist Terror will be the great struggle our lifetime, the great struggle of this century, and I believe we have a moral and strategic obligation to fight it with all tools at our disposal. Just as communism and fascism before it, Islamist extremism is a cancer that must be destroyed.

To blunt their progress, we can begin by coalescing around a comprehensive strategy to wipe out these jihadists and their twisted ideology. Our purpose should be clear: It must be the policy of the United States to confront and defeat Islamist terror groups wherever they are and prevent their reemergence in order to ensure the long-term security of the United States and our allies.

Chairman McCAUL. With that, I recognize the Ranking Member.

Mr. THOMPSON. I want to thank the Chairman for holding today's hearing. I would also like to welcome Speaker Gingrich back to the House and thank Mr. Jenkins and Mr. Mudd for appearing today.

I am also looking forward to General Hayden's testimony. General Hayden, as you know, over the weekend the United States pulled its remaining personnel out of Yemen due to a dire security situation in that country. There have been some who criticized the decision to pull out of Yemen, claiming that pulling out of Yemen in the interest of security puts other foreign intelligence at risk.

I want to learn from you when it is appropriate to leave our public servants in a dangerous situation in the interest of gathering more intelligence.

This hearing is the latest in a series of committee activities relating to combating ideological extremism. Last month, the Chairman and I announced a bipartisan task force on the threat from foreign fighters. That task force commenced its work on March 2.

In last month's full committee hearing on the threat from foreign fighters, the director of the National Counterterrorism Center, Nicholas Rasmussen, stated that more work remains to ensure that our foreign partners are willing and able to identify and stop foreign fighters at their borders. I look forward to the task force's recommendation.

Also the committee Democrats have also asked the Government Accountability Office to look into the Obama's administration's counter violent extremism strategy. Further, it is my understanding that the Majority staff is doing an examination of the strategy.

Mr. Chairman, as we continue to examine the threat from home-grown terrorism, it is my hope that in the future we hold a hearing to learn from the administration how its strategy empowering local partners to prevent violent extremism will be helpful. While I understand that the White House held a summit last month on violent extremism, this strategy has been in place since 2011. It is past time that Members hear from the administration on this topic.

Threats from foreign and domestic terrorist groups are not going away overnight. For years we have seen how terrorist groups use the internet and social media to recruit new members and spread their ideology. It is not surprising that social media is being used to espouse messages of fear and terror, to cultivate extreme viewpoints and inspire terrorists.

These outlets are inexpensive and far-reaching, enabling any extremist group to take advantage of them. A quick search of the internet can produce content from extremists of all stripes, from neo-Nazis to ISIL sympathizers to those who have pledged allegiance to al-Qaeda. Last month Director Rasmussen also stated that ISIL's exploitation of social media played a prominent role in the group's ability to recruit fighters from around the world.

As we find ways to counter terrorist messages at home, we do not focus on one specific ethnic, age, religious, or gender group. The range of indictments and prosecutions from the Department of Justice, from last week's indictment of a 47-year-old Air Force veteran to the indictment of a 21-year-old man from Southern California, to the sentencing of a 19-year-old girl from Colorado to the sentencing of a 44-year-old man from North Carolina illustrates that the number of Americans seeking association with ISIL is diverse.

Mr. Chairman, an unfortunate reality we know all too well but do not want to face is a successful lone-wolf attack inspired by a terrorist group on American soil. I want to build upon the work that we are already doing and encourage this committee to continue the serious discussions on ways to counter message while protecting innovations and Constitutional rights. As we consider this threat, we also need to understand how we may use social media to defuse rather than incite.

I look forward to hearing from our witnesses today, and I yield back.

[The statement of Ranking Member Thompson follows:]

STATEMENT OF RANKING MEMBER BENNIE G. THOMPSON

MARCH 24, 2015

Over the weekend, the United States pulled its remaining personnel out of Yemen due to a dire security situation in that country. There have been some who have criticized the decision to pull out of Yemen claiming that pulling out of Yemen in the interest of security puts our foreign intelligence at risk. I want to learn from General Hayden when it is appropriate to leave our public servants in a dangerous situation in the interest of gathering more intelligence.

This hearing is the latest in a series of committee activities related to combating ideological extremism. Last month, the Chairman and I announced a bi-partisan task force on the threat from foreign fighters. That task force commenced its work on March 2.

In last month's full committee hearing on the threat from foreign fighters, the director of the National Counterterrorism Center, Nicholas Rasmussen, stated that more work remains to ensure that our foreign partners are willing and able to identify and stop foreign fighters at their borders. I look forward to the task force's recommendations. Also, the committee Democrats have also asked the Government Accountability Office to look into the Obama administration's Counter Violent Extremism Strategy.

Further, it is my understanding that the Majority staff is doing an examination of the strategy. As we continue to examine the threat from home-grown terrorism, it is my hope that in the future we hold a hearing to learn from the administration how its strategy, "Empowering Local Partners to Prevent Violent Extremism", will be helpful. While I understand that the White House held a summit last month on violent extremism, this strategy has been in place since 2011. It is past time that Members hear from the administration on this topic.

Threats from foreign and domestic terrorist groups are not going away overnight. For years, we have seen how terrorist groups use the internet and social media to recruit new members and spread their ideology. It is not surprising that social media is being used to espouse messages of fear and terror; to cultivate extreme viewpoints; and to inspire terrorists. These outlets are inexpensive and far-reaching, enabling any extremist group to take advantage of them.

A quick search of the internet can produce content from extremists of all stripes— from Neo Nazis to ISIL sympathizers to those who have pledged allegiance to al-Qaeda. Last month, Director Rasmussen also stated that ISIL's exploitation of social media played a prominent role in the group's ability to recruit fighters from around the world. As we find ways to counter the terrorist's messages at home, we do not focus on one specific ethnic, age, religious, or gender group.

The range of indictments and prosecutions from the Department of Justice—from last week's indictment of a 47-year-old Air Force veteran to the indictment of a 21-year-old man from Southern California to the sentencing of a 19-year-old girl from Colorado to sentencing of a 44-year-old man from North Carolina—illustrates that the number of Americans seeking association with ISIL is diverse. None of the people that the Department of Justice has charged with providing material support to ISIL has been charged with plotting an attack in the United States.

An unfortunate reality we know all too well, but do not want to face, is a successful lone-wolf attack inspired by a terrorist group on American soil. I want to build upon the work that we are already doing and encourage this committee to continue the serious discussions on ways to countermessage while protecting innovation and Constitutional rights. As we consider this real threat, we also need to understand how we may use social media to diffuse rather than incite.

Chairman McCAUL. Thank the Ranking Member. Other Members are reminded that statements may be submitted for the record.

[The statement of Hon. Jackson Lee follows:]

STATEMENT OF HONORABLE SHEILA JACKSON LEE

MARCH 24, 2015

I thank Chairman McCaul and Ranking Member Thompson for holding this morning's hearing on "A Global Battlefield: The Fight Against Islamist Extremism at Home and Abroad."

I welcome and thank today's witnesses: The Honorable Newt Gingrich, former Speaker of the U.S. House of Representatives; General Michael Hayden (USAF–Ret.) the former director of the Central Intelligence Agency as well as the former director of the National Security Agency; Mr. Philip Mudd, senior fellow, New America Foundation; and Mr. Brian Michael Jenkins, a senior adviser to the RAND President of The RAND Corporation.

As a senior Member of this committee and former chair of the Homeland Security's Subcommittee on Transportation Security my commitment to air travel security and protecting the homeland from terrorist attacks remains unwavering.

Since September 11, 2001, it has been a priority of this Nation to prevent terrorists or those who would do Americans harm from boarding flights whether they are domestic or international.

To succeed in the fight against violent extremism defined by the actions of ISIS/ISIL and Boko Haram we must use every asset available to stop the spread of the violence they perpetrate as well as their ability to find safe havens in areas where Government authority is not enforced or consistent.

The battle against violent extremism is constantly changing and it is good to see in General Hayden's testimony that reality.

In recent days we have seen the conditions in Yemen fall into chaos as violent extremism-inspired attacks have claimed the lives of hundreds of worshipers attending prayer services at Mosques.

General Hayden's assessment that no one should second-guess decisions of military leaders and the President to withdraw troops from Yemen because they are in the best position to know all of the facts is correct.

Today's witnesses testify that we are in a new era of geo-political conflict.

It is no longer a matter of governments fielding armies or combatants—but the emergence of what is best described as a new form of geo-military transnational gang activity.

The affiliations of violent extremists individuals and groups are loose with membership remaining fluid—one individual or small group may identify with al-Qaeda today, and switch its identification to ISIL or al-Shabaab or Boko Haram depending on which group is perceived to be the strongest.

These groups require chaos to function and they attack institutions and people regardless of their religious or ethnic traditions to destabilize regions.

They act in the name of religion but institute intra- and inter-Muslim faith conflicts against individuals and mosques to kill thousands.

Violent extremism is not new—those who struggle to hold onto an idyllic past or rigid view of their faith that does not tolerate non-conformism has plagued societies throughout history.

The only tools that have succeed in overcoming violent extremism is the commitment of those most affected by their violence to stand against them.

In the case of ISIS/ISIL the boots on the ground needed to defeat them must be Egyptian, Jordanian, Saudi Arabian, Kurdish, Peshmerga with the full support of United States resources.

I firmly believe that the most important lesson over the last decade is that the United States can want many things for the peoples of the impacted region, but it is the people in the impacted regions who must win these victories for themselves.

We must remember that after the battles are all fought and decided that the underlying causes for so many willing souls to commit themselves to kill and die for ISIS/ISIL and Boko Haram must be addressed.

Where there is poverty, corruption, a sense of not having value or social worth, violence and systemic disparity in living conditions and insurmountable forces to resist upward mobility by poor communities lays fertile ground for recruiting training and turning young minds toward violence.

Some would argue that these problems are not ours to solve.

The counter argument is that the cost of not solving these underlying problems makes the ability to win a lasting end to violent extremism nearly impossible.

We cannot kill ideas with bombs—we must change hearts and minds.

I am a firm supporter of getting to the source of problems that come from the complexity of our interconnected world.

Part of the struggle for peace we have today is a direct consequence of invading Iraq without provocation or reason.

Paraphrasing Secretary of State Colin Powell's advice to President George W. Bush: ''If we break it—we will own it.''

He was warning President Bush about the folly of entering into a war of choice with Iraq and the complexities of that region of the world that could spiral out of control.

It is time that we recognize how right Secretary Powell was then and how his words are playing out every day.

Added to the challenge of violent extremism is its ability to very effectively use the tools of social media to reach far beyond the battlefield to influence young people to join their cause.

Our work as Members of this committee should focus on ensuring that the Department of Homeland Security has the resources needed to meet the challenges presented for violent extremism.

I thank today's witnesses and look forward to their testimony.

Thank you.

Chairman McCAUL. We are fortunate to have a very distinguished panel before us here today. First, Speaker Newt Gingrich served as Speaker of the House of Representatives from 1995 to 1999. He served the sixth district of Georgia in the House for 20 years, and he is currently a contributor to CNN. Thank you, sir, for being here today.

Next we have General Michael Hayden. He is a principal at the Chertoff Group. Served as the director of the Central Intelligence Agency from 2006 to 2009 and as director of the National Security

Agency from 1999 to 2005 and held a variety of other posts during his 41-year Air Force career. Thank you, sir, as well.

Mr. Philip Mudd is a senior research fellow at the New America Foundation. He served in the Central Intelligence Agency for 20 years, including as deputy director of the agency's Counterterrorism Center from 2003 to 2005, and he also served in the FBI's National security branch. Thank you, sir.

Then finally we have Mr. Brian Jenkins. He is a senior advisor to the president of the RAND Corporation, served as an advisor to the White House commission on aviation safety and security and advised the National commission on terrorism in 2000. Previously also served in the United States Army. Thank you, sir, for being here as well.

The Chairman now recognizes Mr. Gingrich.

STATEMENTS OF HON. NEWT GINGRICH, FORMER SPEAKER OF THE U.S. HOUSE OF REPRESENTATIVES

Mr. GINGRICH. Thank you, Chairman McCaul and Ranking Member Thompson, and all the Members of the committee for holding this very important hearing. I am glad that you have begun a process of fundamental rethinking which a number of other committees will have to emulate. It is vital that the United States Congress undertake a thorough no-holds-barred review of the long global war in which we are now engaged with radical Islamists.

This review will require a number of committees to coordinate, since it will have to include Intelligence, Armed Services, Foreign Affairs, Judiciary, and Homeland Security at a minimum.

There are three key sobering observations about where we are today which should force this thorough, no-holds-barred review of our situation. These three points, which I think are backed up by the facts, suggest that the United States is drifting into a crisis that could challenge its very survival over time.

First, it is the case that after 35 years of conflict, dating back to the Iranian seizure of the American Embassy in Tehran and the ensuing hostage crisis, the United States and its allies are losing the long global war with radical Islamists. We are losing to both the violent jihad and to the cultural jihad. The violent jihad has shown itself recently in Paris, Australia, Tunisia, Syria, Iraq, Libya, Egypt, Gaza, Nigeria, Somalia, Afghanistan, and Yemen, to name just some of the most prominent areas of violence.

Cultural jihad is more insidious and in many ways more dangerous. Cultural jihad strikes at our very ability to think and have an honest dialogue about the steps necessary for our survival.

Cultural jihad is winning when the Department of Defense describes a terrorist attack at Fort Hood as workplace violence.

Cultural jihad is winning when the President refers to random killings in Paris, when they were clearly the actions of Islamist terrorists and targeted against specific groups.

Cultural jihad is winning when the administration censors training documents and lecturers according to sensitivity so that they cannot describe radical Islamists with any reference to the religious ideology which is the primary bond that unites them.

In the 14 years since the 9/11 attacks, we have gone a long way down the road of intellectually and morally disarming in order to appease the cultural jihadists who are increasingly aggressive in asserting their right to define how the rest of us think and talk.

Second, it is the case that in an extraordinarily dangerous pattern our intelligence system has been methodically limited and manipulated to sustain false narratives while suppressing or rejecting facts and analysis about those who would kill us. For example, there is clear evidence the American people have been given remarkably misleading analysis about al-Qaeda based on a very limited translation and publication of about 24 of the 1.5 million documents captured in the bin Laden raid.

A number of outside analysts have suggested that the selective release of a small number of documents was designed to make the case that al-Qaeda was weaker. These outside analysts assert that a broader reading of more documents would indicate al-Qaeda was doubling in size when our Government claimed it was getting weaker, an analysis also supported by obvious empirical facts on the ground.

Furthermore, there has been what could only be deliberate foot-dragging and exploiting this extraordinary cache of material. Both Lieutenant General Mike Flynn, the former head of the Defense Intelligence Agency, and Colonel Derek Harvey, a leading analyst of terrorism, have described the deliberately misleading and restricted access to the bin Laden documents. A number of intelligence operatives have described censorship from above designed to make sure that intelligence which undermines the official narrative simply does not see the light of day.

Congress should explore legislation which would make it illegal to instruct intelligence personnel to falsify information or analysis. Basing American security policy on politically-defined distortions of reality is a very dangerous habit which could someday lead to a devastating defeat. Congress has an obligation to ensure the American people are learning the truth and have an opportunity to debate potential policies in a fact-based environment.

Third, it is the case that our political elites have refused to define our enemies. Their willful ignorance has made it impossible to develop an effective strategy to defeat those who would destroy our civilization. For example, the President's own press secretary engages in verbal gymnastics to avoid identifying the perpetrators of violence as radical Islamists.

Josh Earnest says such labels do not, ''accurately describe our enemies'' and that to use such a label, ''legitimizes them.'' This is Orwellian doublespeak. The radical Islamists do not need to be delegitimized. They need to be defeated. We cannot defeat what we cannot name.

There has been a desperate desire among our elites to focus on the act of terrorism rather than the motivation behind these acts. There has been a deep desire to avoid the cultural and religious motivation behind the jihadist factions.

Let me conclude because of time. I think it is very important that we recognize that there are ties between Minneapolis and Mogadishu. There are ties between London, Paris, and ISIS. Al-Qaeda exists in many forms and under many names. We are confronted by world-wide recruiting on the internet, with Islamists reaching out to people we would never have imagined were vulnerable to that kind of support.

We have been refusing to apply the insights and lessons of history, but our enemies have been very willing to study, learn, and rethink them. Until we reverse this, we will not in fact be capable of winning this war.

[The prepared statement of Hon. Gingrich follows:]

PREPARED STATEMENT OF HONORABLE NEWT GINGRICH

MARCH 24, 2015

Thank you Chairman McCaul and Ranking Member Thompson and all the Members of the committee for holding this very important hearing.

I am glad that you have begun a process of fundamental rethinking which a number of other committees will have to emulate.

It is vital that the United States Congress undertake a thorough, no-holds-barred review of the long, global war in which we are now engaged with radical Islamists. This review will require a number of committees to coordinate since it will have to include Intelligence, Armed Services, Foreign Affairs, Judiciary, and Homeland Security at a minimum.

There are three key, sobering observations about where we are today which should force this thorough, no-holds-barred review of our situation.

These three points—which are backed up by the facts—suggest the United States is drifting into a crisis that could challenge its very survival.

First, it is the case that after 35 years of conflict dating back to the Iranian seizure of the American Embassy in Tehran and the ensuing hostage crisis, the United States and its allies are losing the long, global war with radical Islamists.

We are losing to both the violent Jihad and to the cultural Jihad.

The violent Jihad has shown itself recently in Paris, Australia, Tunisia, Syria, Iraq, Libya, Egypt, Gaza, Nigeria, Somalia, Afghanistan, and Yemen to name just some of the most prominent areas of violence.

Cultural Jihad is more insidious and in many ways more dangerous. Cultural Jihad strikes at our very ability to think and to have an honest dialogue about the steps necessary for our survival. Cultural Jihad is winning when the Department of Defense describes a terrorist attack at Fort Hood as ''workplace violence''.[1] Cultural Jihad is winning when the President refers to ''random'' killings in Paris when they were clearly the actions of Islamist terrorists and targeted against specific groups.[2] Cultural Jihad is winning when the administration censors training documents and lecturers according to ''sensitivity'' so that they cannot describe radical Islamists with any reference to the religious ideology which is the primary bond that unites them.[3]

In the 14 years since the 9/11 attacks, we have gone a long way down the road of intellectually and morally disarming in order to appease the cultural Jihadists who are increasingly aggressive in asserting their right to define how the rest of us think and talk.

Second, it is the case that, in an extraordinarily dangerous pattern, our intelligence system has been methodically limited and manipulated to sustain false narratives while suppressing or rejecting facts and analysis about those who would kill us.

For example, there is clear evidence the American people have been given remarkably misleading analysis about al-Qaeda based on a very limited translation and publication of about 24 of the 1.5 million documents captured in the bin Laden raid. A number of outside analysts have suggested that the selective release of a small number of documents was designed to make the case that al-Qaeda was weaker.[4] These outside analysts assert that a broader reading of more documents would indi-

---

[1] Department of Defense Press Release, August 20, 2010, *http://www.defense.gov/news/newsarticle.aspx?id=60536.*

[2] President Obama, Interview with Vox News, February 2015, *http://www.vox.com/a/barack-obama-interview-vox-conversation/obama-foreign-policy-transcript.*

[3] Deputy Attorney General James M. Cole Speaks at the Department's Conference on Post-9/11 Discrimination, October 19, 2011 *http://www.justice.gov/opa/speech/deputy-attorney-gen- eral-james-m-cole-speaks-department-s-conference-post-911.*

[4] Stephen Hayes and Thomas Joscelyn, ''How America Was Mislead on al Qaeda's Demise,'' Wall Street Journal, March 5, 2015; *http://www.wsj.com/articles/stephen-hayes-and-tomas-joscelyn-how-america-was-misled-on-al-qaedas-demise-1425600796.*

cate al-Qaeda was doubling in size when our Government claimed it was getting weaker—an analysis also supported by obvious empirical facts on the ground. Furthermore, there has been what could only be deliberate foot-dragging in exploiting this extraordinary cache of material.

Both Lt. General Mike Flynn, the former head of the Defense Intelligence Agency, and Colonel Derek Harvey, a leading analyst of terrorism, have described the deliberately misleading and restricted access to the bin Laden documents.

A number of intelligence operatives have described censorship from above designed to make sure that intelligence which undermines the official narrative simply does not see the light of day.[5]

Congress should explore legislation which would make it illegal to instruct intelligence personnel to falsify information or analysis. Basing American security policy on politically-defined distortions of reality is a very dangerous habit which could someday lead to a devastating defeat. Congress has an obligation to ensure the American people are learning the truth and have an opportunity to debate potential policies in a fact-based environment.

Third, it is the case that our political elites have refused to define our enemies. Their willful ignorance has made it impossible to develop an effective strategy to defeat those who would destroy our civilization.

For example, the President's own press secretary engages in verbal gymnastics to avoid identifying the perpetrators of violence as radical Islamists. Josh Earnest said such labels do not ''accurately'' describe our enemies and that to use such a label ''legitimizes'' them.[6]

This is Orwellian double-speak. The radical Islamists do not need to be de-legitimized. They need to be defeated. We cannot defeat what we cannot name.

There has been a desperate desire among our elites to focus on the act of terrorism rather than the motivation behind those acts. There has been a deep desire to avoid the cultural and religious motivations behind the Jihadists' actions. There is an amazing hostility to any effort to study or teach the history of these patterns going back to the Seventh Century.

Because our elites refuse to look at the religious and historic motivations and patterns which drive our opponents, we are responding the same way to attack after attack on our way of life without any regard for learning about what really motivates our attackers. Only once we learn what drives and informs our opponents will we not repeat the same wrong response tactics, groundhog day-like, and finally start to win this long war.

Currently each new event, each new group, each new pattern is treated as though it's an isolated phenomenon—as if it's not part of a larger struggle with a long history and deep roots in patterns that are 1,400 years old.

There is a passion for narrowing and localizing actions. The early focus was al-Qaeda. Then it was the Taliban. Now it is ISIS. It is beginning to be Boko Harum. As long as the elites can keep treating each new eruption as a free-standing phenomenon, they can avoid having to recognize that this is a global, world-wide movement that is decentralized but not disordered.

There are ties between Minneapolis and Mogadishu.[7] There are ties between London, Paris, and ISIS. Al-Qaeda exists in many forms and under many names. We are confronted by world-wide recruiting on the internet, with Islamists reaching out to people we would never have imagined were vulnerable to that kind of appeal.

We have been refusing to apply the insights and lessons of history but our enemies have been very willing to study, learn, rethink, and evolve.

The cultural Jihadists have learned our language and our principles—freedom of speech, freedom of religion, tolerance—and they apply them to defeat us without believing in them themselves. We blindly play their game on their terms, and don't even think about how absurd it is for people who accept no church, no synagogue, no temple, in their heartland to come into our society and define multicultural sensitivity totally to their advantage—meaning, in essence, that we cannot criticize their ideas.

Our elites have been morally and intellectually disarmed by their own unwillingness to look at both the immediate history of the first 35 years of the global war

---

[5] Eli Lake, '' 'Over My Dead Body': Spies Fight Obama Push to Downsize Terror War,'' The Daily Beast, May 21, 2015; *http://www.thedailybeast.com/articles/2014/05/21/over-my-dead-body-spies-fight-obama-push-to-downsize-terror-war.html*.

[6] John Earnest, Press Conference, January 13, 2015, *https://www.whitehouse.gov/the-press-office/2015/01/13/press-briefing-press-secretary-josh-earnest-1132015*.

[7] CBS News, ''Minneapolis has become a recruiting ground for Islamic extremists'', August 27, 2014; *http://www.cbsnews.com/news/minneapolis-has-become-recruiting-ground-for-islamic-extremists/*.

with radical Islamists and then to look deeper into the roots of the ideology and the military-political system our enemies draw upon as their guide to waging both physical and cultural warfare.

One of the great threats to American independence is the steady growth of foreign money pouring into our intellectual and political systems to influence our thinking and limit our options for action. Congress needs to adopt new laws to protect the United States from the kind of foreign influences which are growing in size and boldness.

Sun Tzu, in the Art of War, written 500 years before Christ, warned that ''all warfare is based on deception''. We are currently in a period where our enemies are deceiving us—and our elites are actively deceiving themselves—and us. The deception and dishonesty of our elites is not accidental or uninformed. It is deliberate and willful. The flow of foreign money and foreign influence is a significant part of that pattern of deception.

We must clearly define our enemies before we can begin to develop strategies to defeat them.

We have lost 35 years since this war began.

We are weaker and our enemies are stronger.

Congress has a duty to pursue the truth and to think through the strategies needed and the structures which will be needed to implement those strategies.

Thank you for this opportunity to discuss the dangers we face.

I look forward to your questions.

Chairman McCAUL. Thank you, Mr. Speaker. The Chairman now recognizes General Hayden.

STATEMENT OF MICHAEL V. HAYDEN, (USAF–RET.), FORMER DIRECTOR, CENTRAL INTELLIGENCE AGENCY, AND FORMER DIRECTOR, NATIONAL SECURITY AGENCY

General HAYDEN. Thank you, Chairman McCaul and Ranking Member Thompson, for the invitation. Let me also thank the entire committee for taking on what is a difficult but very important topic. We are engaged in a global battlefield, fighting against those who would commit violence on the innocent for their own warped objectives. There is much to be said about the battlefield, and I am sure we will be talking in great detail about it as we go forward today.

But I also know we cannot have an honest discussion of that without also discussing one of the world's great monotheisms. So before I launch into that let me say that I understand that Islam, Christianity, and Judaism all trace their roots back to the same deserts, that we are all people of the book and that we are all children of Abraham. But we cannot conduct, as the Speaker just noted, we cannot conduct a useful discussion of the current conflict without also talking about Islam.

We are not talking about all of Islam. We are certainly not talking about all Muslims, but we risk confusing ourselves if we ignore the religious roots that some use to justify their violence.

If you look at the current conflict in the Levant, ISIS and so on, there are actually three wars going on there simultaneously. The first is an intra-Sunni battle. In one case one group of Sunni terrorists, ISIS, against another group, al-Qaeda. In another it is Sunni-based violent extremism against the Sunni states in the region, so it is ISIS Jordan, ISIS Egypt, ISIS against Saudi Arabia. It is all Sunni on Sunni, with Sunni fundamentalists trying to construct an Islamic caliphate at the expense of traditional Muslim states.

Second conflict, Sunni-Shia, which is unfortunately the continuation of the succession crisis that began at the death of the Prophet in 632. Here we have the so-called Shia crescent—Iran, large portions of Iraq, the Alawites in Syria, Hezbollah in Lebanon—against the Sunni monarchies in states like Egypt. Frankly, the worst of the current violence we are seeing like, as you mentioned, Mr. Chairman, the mass bombings in Yemen, reflect the Sunni-Shia conflict. I suspect that is going to take on an increasingly powerful flavor for the violence in the Middle East.

The third conflict is the challenge of reconciling Islam with what we in the West at least call modernity. I want to avoid cultural arrogance here, since Christendom went through a similar crisis in the 17th Century. But at the end of the Thirty Years War then we in Europe broadly decided to separate the sacred from the secular in our political cultures. I know that is an oversimplification but it is instructive, and that outcome has led to a growth of religious tolerance that has characterized at least the best of Western life since then.

It remains to be seen whether or not another great monotheism, Islam, follows that same arc, or if religion there will remain the business of the state, or in its extreme form, replace the state.

Now the common thread across those three conflicts within Sunni Islam, Sunni-Shia, and Islam and modernity, the common thread is Islam. Richard Haas, the chairman of the Council on Foreign Relations, has compared the current conflict to the Thirty Years War in Europe. I fear that he is correct and, Mr. Chairman, what we are seeing here is going to last a generation or more.

I know that a lot has been made about recent administration comments that what we really have here is a lack of opportunity and these issues could be solved by more jobs and better economic development, and actually there is truth to that. When I was at CIA I was fond of saying that many jihadists join the movement for the same reasons that some young Americans join the Crips and the Bloods. There is much here about youthful alienation, the need to belong to something greater than self, the search for meaningful identity. But it also matters what gang you join, and this gang at its senior levels justifies its horrific violence through reference to the holy Quoran.

Mr. Chairman, it is fundamentally a struggle over ideas. Unfortunately, it is a struggle over which we, as a largely Judeo-Christian nation, have only limited influence. We can try to set the conditions for success, we could try to empower and protect moderate voices. But we also have to look to our own safety by resorting to force to kill or capture those who are already committed to do us violence.

But in the long term the only solution for this lies within Islam itself, and here a recent speech by President Sisi of Egypt to the scholars at El Azhar University, the seat of Sunni scholarship, is incredibly encouraging. In essence the President of Egypt told the theologians that they have to get their act together and correct and discredit what he views to be gross misinterpretations of Islamic scripture by the jihadists.

By the way, he also attended mass and wished his Coptic fellow citizens Merry Christmas. President Sisi is an observant, pious Muslim, so his words and his action should carry some weight and also offer us some hope.

Mr. Chairman, there is a lot more to be said about this and I look forward to the committee's questions.

[The prepared statement of General Hayden follows:]

PREPARED STATEMENT OF MICHAEL V. HAYDEN

MARCH 24, 2015

Thank you Chairman McCaul and Ranking Member Thompson for the invitation to be here today. Let me also thank the entire committee for taking on this difficult, but very important topic.

We are truly engaged on a global battlefield fighting against those who would visit violence on the innocent for their own warped objectives.

There is much to be said about this battlefield and I am sure we will discuss the roots of the violent extremism which we now face.

And I know we cannot have an honest discussion of that without also discussing one of the world's great monotheisms. So before I launch into that, let me say that I understand that Islam, Christianity, and Judaism all trace their roots to the same deserts. That we are all people of the book. And that we are all children of Abraham.

But we cannot conduct a useful discussion of our current conflict without also talking about Islam. In my view, we are not talking about all of Islam and we certainly are not talking about all Muslims, but we risk confusing ourselves if we ignore the religious roots that some use to justify their violence.

In looking at the current conflict in the Levant, there are actually three wars going on simultaneously.

The first is an intra-Sunni battle, in one case pitting Isis against al-Qaeda. In another case, it is Sunni-based violent extremists against the Sunni states in the region. Here we see Isis against Jordan. Isis against Egypt. Isis against Saudi Arabia. This is all Sunni-on-Sunni, with Sunni fundamentalists trying to construct an Islamic caliphate at the expense of traditional Muslim states.

The second conflict is Sunni-Shia, the continuation of a succession crisis following the death of the prophet that began in 632. Here we have the so-called Shia Crescent—Iran, much of Iraq, the Alawites in Syria, and Hezballah in Lebanon—against the Sunni monarchies and states like Egypt. The worst of the current violence we are seeing, like the horrific mosque bombings in Yemen, reflect this conflict. And I think we will see this conflict becoming more dominant and more violent as we go forward.

The third conflict is the challenge of reconciling Islam with what we in the West call modernity. I want to avoid cultural arrogance here, Mr. Chairman, since Christendom went through a similar crisis in the 17th Century. And at the end of the Thirty Years War then, we in Europe broadly decided to separate the sacred from the secular in our political cultures. I know that that is an oversimplification, but it is instructive. That outcome has led to a growth of religious tolerance that has characterized the best of Western life since. It remains to be seen whether or not another great monotheism, Islam, will follow this same arc or if religion there will remain the business of state or—in its extreme form—replace the state.

The common thread across these three conflicts is Islam. And indeed, Richard Haass, the chairman of the Council on Foreign Relations, has compared the current conflict in the Levant to Europe's Thirty Years War. I fear that he is correct and what we are seeing here will last a generation or more.

I know that much has been made about recent administration comments that what we really have here is a lack of opportunity and that these issues could be solved by more jobs and better economic development.

There is actually truth to that. When at CIA I was fond of saying that many jihadists join the movement for the same reasons that some young Americans join the Crips and the Bloods. There is much here about youthful alienation, the need to belong to something greater than self, the search for meaningful identity. But it also matters what gang you join. And this gang, at its senior levels, justifies its horrific violence through references to the holy Quran.

This is fundamentally a struggle over ideas, and unfortunately it is a struggle over which we, as largely a Judeo-Christian nation, have only limited influence. We can try to set the conditions for success, by empowering and protecting moderate voices, for example. We also have to look to our own safety by resorting to force to kill or capture those already committed to doing us violence.

But over the long term, the only solution lies within Islam itself. Here, the recent speech by President Sisi of Egypt to the scholars al Azhar University, the seat of

Sunni scholarship, is most encouraging. In essence, the president told the theologians that they have to get their act together and correct and discredit what he views to be gross misinterpretations of Islamic scripture by the jihadists.

Sisi also attended Mass and wished his Coptic fellow citizens Merry Christmas.

President Sisi is an observant, pious Muslim so his words and his actions should carry some weight and offer us some hope.

Mr. Chairman, there is a lot more to be said about this topic and I look forward to the committee's questions.

Chairman MCCAUL. Thank you, General. The Chairman now recognizes Mr. Mudd.

STATEMENT OF PHILIP MUDD, SENIOR FELLOW, NEW AMERICA FOUNDATION

Mr. MUDD. Thank you. I was calculating that I think I sat through maybe 2,000 threat briefings between 2001 and 2010 at the FBI and CIA, so let me sketch that story and bring it to today. Those first briefings I sat in, we had an adversary, an enemy that was geographically concentrated, Afghanistan, Pakistan. We had a clear partner, that was largely the Pakistanis, extending to people like the Saudis, but a lot of the action was in the tribal areas of Pakistan.

Recruitment by the adversary was done personally. The 19 hijackers had personal interaction, either themselves or with their partners within al-Qaeda organization, and we owned the data. Silicon Valley didn't.

Let's transition quickly. If you look at the intervening years, we went from Afghanistan and Pakistan. I remember the threat briefings about the beheading of an American in Saudi Arabia back in about 2003. We had attacks against tourists and embassies in Indonesia back in that time frame. We transitioned to foreign fighters going into Iraq.

I moved to the Bureau. We had Somali kids, first-generation in Minneapolis, Minnesota, going out to Somalia. We went back to Iraq and today we talk about Nigeria. So the geographic space has changed radically in the 14 years.

Let me take you back to the story of the threat table and transition to where we are today and draw a contrast. We don't have a geographic location. We have got Africa, we have got Tunisia, we have got Somalia, Yemen, Iraq. The Indonesians and the Filipinos have done okay, but I am not sure they will do okay forever.

We don't have a single partner. We have got partners in Mali and Cameroon, in Nigeria. We have got partners in the African Union. We have lost partners in Yemen, so the partnerships are going to change radically as the geography and the adversary changes.

The adversary is recruiting not personally but digitally. We did not face this at the threat table in 2001, 2002, 2003. We didn't. We don't own the data. PayPal does, Google does, Verizon does.

So let me offer you a suggestion, a handful of suggestions on how we handle not only a conflict that has changed rapidly in the story that I just told you but a conflict that I can tell you as an expert analyst, I don't know where it is going to go tomorrow. Anybody who says here is the geographic space and here is the partner in 2016, throw them out. They don't know.

No. 1, we are going to have to be agile. Look at what the French did in Mali a few years ago. Small footprint, special forces, intelligence support, partnership with local security services, and think about bringing in the CIA and the military to talk about not where the geography is—we don't know—but how do we ensure they are enabled for rapid movement against a rapid adversary?

When you do that, let me caution you, there is going to be human rights problems. If you think that is theoretical, we deal with it today in Iraq and we are dealing with it in Nigeria. These are the partners who are fighting the adversaries. These partners are dirty and the partners of the future will be. So when we think about enabling them, we are going to step into it.

Next, and let me close on this. The cyber issue, which I know is critically important to a lot of you, and in the past few years I have been out of Government and talked to the cyber folks, talked to Silicon Valley. Not only do we not own the data, the U.S. Government is not well-positioned, nor will it ever be, to own a conversation in a democratic society about a religion that is not part of our Judeo-Christian heritage. We don't own the concepts. Furthermore, I don't think we have the agility to respond to an adversary that moves as quickly as this adversary does.

I think we need a different engagement in the digital space. None of this engagement, in my view, should be led by the U.S. Government. It should be enabled by the U.S. Government. Let me give you two examples.

The scenarios I see for recruitment on the internet. A 15-year-old girl, for example in Denver, talks to somebody on Facebook, maybe sees something on Twitter, maybe sees something in Instagram. The scenarios we worry about there, the age of the child, the travel routes, the way data moves, the way that individual interacts with the internet. We should be creating scenarios that we talk about with the owners of the data in Silicon Valley. What I am talking about is having working groups and saying, this is what we are seeing in the digital space. You own the space. What would you recommend we do and what are you worried about in terms of law and policy?

''What should we do?'' is the question that we should be posing to Silicon Valley and not necessarily telling them how we are going to resolve this.

Finally, when we fight this I think we should be enabling people who are already in this space. Let me give you one example. Women are powerful in this game because families are being destroyed. Increasingly those women have smart phones. If you look at smart phone usage and how smart phone usage will change in the Arabian Peninsula, in north Africa, remarkable.

We should be talking also to NGOs, for example, about how we open doors in places like Africa and Central Asia. Bring in Yahoo, bring in Twitter. What do you need to do to ensure that women get on-line and start talking about how violence is destroying families? I am not saying that is the only solution. All I am saying is in the examples I gave you in the digital space, the U.S. Government doesn't own the data and they don't own the action.

Just a few thoughts. I think I am 1 second over.

[The prepared statement of Mr. Mudd follows:]

PREPARED STATEMENT OF PHILIP MUDD

MARCH 24, 2015

The terror battleground has undergone a revolution during the 14 years after the 9/11 attacks. Among the most significant changes intelligence community agencies face are the rapid spread of the physical geography of terrorism and the virtual geography of terror propaganda, radicalization, and recruitment.

When I returned to the CIA from a White House assignment in January 2002, the CIA Counterterrorist Center faced a clear terror target: The architects of the 9/11 attacks. Most of those al-Qaeda terrorists fled from Afghanistan to Pakistan—though some went to Iran—and their geographic footprint was small; overall, the al-Qaeda organization was not large. Before 9/11, though, the dissemination of the al-Qaeda message had spread across the globe, as far afield as East Asia, North Africa, and Western Europe. The methods of disseminating that message had not yet entered the internet age. Today, like the rapid spread of the locations in which al-Qaeda-inspired groups operate, the virtual efforts by these groups have ridden the internet and social media wave. What was once an al-Qaeda group is now an al-Qaedist revolution.

Both these stories, then—the physical reach of violent extremism and its virtual influence—have changed, and they continue to evolve quickly:

- We do not have an adversary's leadership that operates within one clearly-defined geographic area. The al-Qaedist revolution, now morphed into the new and different ISIS ideology, includes leadership and groupings in areas as far-flung as northern Nigeria, Libya, Syria, Iraq, Yemen, and the West.
- We cannot target individuals who are radicalization nodes; now, the nodes are virtual, difficult to trace, and easily altered, sheltered, or moved by the adversary.

We can talk about the evolution of these changes and the emerging virtual nodes, but we might consider focusing as well on how we respond to them, in both the public and private sectors. Following are a few questions we might consider discussing during the hearing on 24 March:

- What kind of public/private partnerships might we consider as we enter an era in which private companies—phone, internet, shopping, and other digitally-driven firms—hold information that can help locate, track, and apprehend adversaries?
- How should the U.S. Government engage with NGOs and private-sector companies in developing strategies to counter this ideology? Should the Government lead or follow?

Thank you for inviting me to the hearing. I look forward to the conversation about the future of counterterrorism, and the future of intelligence and Federal law enforcement in the digital age.

Chairman MCCAUL. Thank you, Mr. Mudd.

Mr. Jenkins is recognized.

STATEMENT OF BRIAN MICHAEL JENKINS, SENIOR ADVISER TO THE RAND PRESIDENT, THE RAND CORPORATION

Mr. JENKINS. Chairman McCaul, Ranking Member Thompson, Members of the committee, thank you very much for inviting me to testify on this important issue. Right now the United States confronts a complex and scary matrix of threats. I am going to focus on the threats emanating from the groups in the Middle East.

The civil wars in Syria and Iraq will continue. That is going to sharpen the sectarian divide between Sunnis and Shias. It is going to continue to threaten the stability of the region, and it is going to continue to attract foreign recruits. This goes on.

But neither the rebels arrayed against the Assad regime nor the so-called Islamic State forces in Iraq are going to be able to bring down the governments in Damascus or in Baghdad. But neither government is going to be able to reestablish its authority throughout its territory.

Meanwhile, the surrounding countries and the rest of the world will be dealing with the consequences of these conflicts for many years to come: Humanitarian catastrophe, massive refugee populations, and what has become a terrorist factory.

Two galaxies of jihadist terrorism in the region represent a threat to the U.S. homeland, al-Qaeda and its affiliates, and the Islamic State of Iraq and the Levant. Although the capability of al-Qaeda's core group itself to launch direct attacks on the United States has diminished, al-Qaeda remains committed to attacking us through its affiliates, its allies and home-grown terrorists.

U.S. and British intelligence officials have recently warned that al-Qaeda elements in Syria are also attempting to recruit foreign fighters to mount terrorist attacks in the West right now.

ISIL is a bit different. ISIL has murdered Westerners who have fallen into its hands. It has urged its supporters to carry out terrorist attacks in their own countries. It has applauded them when they have done so. It continues to attract large numbers of Western recruits.

The group right now is preoccupied with expanding and defending its territory. However, ISIL could change its strategy as it loses ground to U.S.-supported offensives. Facing defeat, it could implement a revenge-driven strategy aimed at provoking a final showdown.

Retaking the towns now held by ISIL is certain to be a long and bloody struggle which could scatter fleeing foreign fighters across the planet. Some Westerners will come home seeking refuge or revenge.

Meanwhile, Western governments are faced with a continuing flow of nationals to Syria while trying to intercept those coming back, and that volume is growing.

The good news is that thus far comparatively few Americans are involved in going off to Syria and Iraq, although that number is already more than the total number that tried to go to all of the other jihadists fronts since 9/11.

Western governments also have to deal with the threat of action by frustrated home-grown jihadists who are unable to travel to Syria. Now ISIL's use of deliberate barbaric forms of violence, this resonates with a self-selecting audience of people who are not repelled by such atrocities and may even exert to participate. This is a dangerous bunch.

The last couple of years the terrorist jihad has been distracted by the schism between al-Qaeda and the Islamic State. The two wings of the jihadist movement have even engaged in open warfare in Syria. But these internal divisions have not—have not prevented the spread of jihadist ideology and the establishment of new jihadist footholds. The emergence of the two powerful jihadist adversaries with access to considerable human and financial resources perpetuates the threat. The recent attacks on Western tourists in Tunisia and on Shia mosques in Yemen, both of which were claimed by ISIL, underscore the danger.

Neither side exercises direct control over home-grown jihadists. In fact, some Western jihadists welcome the split, hoping that it will lead to a competition to see which can carry out the more spectacular attacks. The ideology of violent jihad is certainly going to continue. It is going to fuel these regional conflicts while continued exhortation on the internet and intensive media coverage of terrorist attacks like those in Brussels, Ottawa, Sydney, Paris, and Copenhagen are going to excite jihadist fanatics and what we might call jihadist loons.

The most likely threat right now to the United States homeland comes from home-grown terrorists carrying out unsophisticated but lethal assaults. Returning foreign fighters add another layer to the threat, and although international cooperation hopefully has made the terrorists' operating environment a bit more hostile for them, still we have to be willing to accept the risk of more ambitious attempts launched on the United States from abroad. I look forward to your questions.

[The prepared statement of Mr. Jenkins follows:]

PREPARED STATEMENT OF BRIAN MICHAEL JENKINS [1][2]

MARCH 24, 2015

Chairman McCaul, Ranking Member Thompson, distinguished Members of the committee, thank you for inviting me to testify on this important issue.

Homeland security today confronts a complex and scary matrix of threats that range from continued efforts to radicalize and recruit home-grown terrorists to sophisticated cyber attacks on our financial systems and critical infrastructure.

My testimony will focus on the terrorist threat emanating from the conflicts in Syria and Iraq. Here are the key conclusions:

- The civil wars in Syria and Iraq will continue, sharpening the sectarian divide between Sunnis and Shias, threatening the stability of the region, and attracting foreign recruits.
- Neither the rebels arrayed against the Assad regime nor the so-called Islamic State forces in Iraq will be able to bring down the governments in Damascus or Baghdad. But neither government will be able to reestablish its authority throughout its territory.
- For the foreseeable future, Syria will remain a mosaic of ethnic and sectarian enclaves, some under government control, others under rebel control. In Iraq, Iranian-backed Shia militias augmented by regular Iraqi forces and some Sunni militias may push back the Islamic State, but the central government has relinquished military power to militias under control of Iran, Shia clerics, or tribal sheikhs. The Iraqi army is not the dominant member of this assemblage. The territory controlled by Kurdish forces will remain autonomous, if not formally independent. Winning back territory from the Islamic State will not win the loyalty of Iraq's Sunnis. Excesses by Shia militias will guarantee their continued resistance.

The surrounding countries and the rest of the world will be dealing with the consequences of these conflicts—humanitarian catastrophe, massive refugee populations, and a terrorist factory—for many years to come.

There are now two galaxies of jihadist terrorists in the region that represent a credible threat to the U.S. homeland: Al-Qaeda and its affiliates, particularly Al-Qaeda in the Arabian Peninsula (AQAP) in Yemen and Jabhat al-Nusra (JAN) in Syria, and the Islamic State of Iraq and the Levant (ISIL).

The al-Qaeda threat is a continuing one. Although the capability of its core group to launch direct attacks on the United States—the ''far enemy''—has diminished, al-Qaeda remains committed to attacking us through its affiliates, allies, and home-grown terrorists. In the past, AQAP has recruited volunteers and attempted ter-

---

[1] The opinions and conclusions expressed in this testimony are the author's alone and should not be interpreted as representing those of RAND or any of the sponsors of its research. This product is part of the RAND Corporation testimony series. RAND testimonies record testimony presented by RAND associates to Federal, State, or local legislative committees; Government-appointed commissions and panels; and private review and oversight bodies. The RAND Corporation is a nonprofit research organization providing objective analysis and effective solutions that address the challenges facing the public and private sectors around the world. RAND's publications do not necessarily reflect the opinions of its research clients and sponsors.

[2] This testimony is available for free download at *http://www.rand.org/pubs/testimonies/CT429.html*.

rorist attacks on U.S.-bound flights and continues to try to inspire recruits to carry out attacks in the United States. U.S. and British intelligence officials warn that al-Qaeda elements embedded in al-Nusra are also attempting to recruit foreign fighters to mount new terrorist attacks in the West.

ISIL presents a long-term threat. It has brutally murdered Westerners who fell into its hands. It has urged its supporters in the West to carry out terrorist attacks in their own countries and has applauded them when they have done so. And it continues to attract large numbers of Western recruits.

There is no evidence yet that ISIL is planning to launch its own terrorist attacks in the West. It is currently preoccupied with expanding and defending its territory, which is why it needs a continuing flow of foreign volunteers. However, ISIL could change its strategy as it loses ground to U.S.-supported ground offensives. Facing defeat, it could implement a revenge-driven strategy calculated to provoke direct American intervention and a final showdown.

Retaking the cities and towns now held by ISIL is almost certain to be a long, bloody struggle, which could easily turn into a slaughter that scatters fleeing foreign fighters across the planet. Some will join other jihadist fronts; Libya, Yemen, Afghanistan, and the Caucasus are possibilities. Some Westerners will seek refuge—or revenge—at home.

Meanwhile, Western governments, including the United States, are faced with the continued flow of their nationals to Syria and Iraq while trying to intercept those coming back, possibly to carry out individual acts of terrorism. This has already occurred, albeit on a small scale, in Europe.

European authorities are already being overwhelmed by the volume of persons traveling to and from Syria. Thus far, the number of Americans involved appears to be manageable with current resources and laws, although that number is growing. According to official estimates, between 130 and 150 Americans have gone to or attempted to go to Syria in the past 3 years—already more than the total number that have gone to or tried to go to all of the other jihadist fronts since 9/11, a few more than 100.

Western governments must also deal with the threat of action by frustrated home-grown jihadists who are inspired by al-Qaeda's or ISIL's exhortations to action but who are unable to travel to Syria. ISIL's claimed re-creation of the Caliphate has galvanized extremists world-wide. ISIL has also effectively exploited social media to reach a large and impressionable audience.

ISIL's use of deliberately barbaric forms of violence—mass executions, beheadings, crucifixions, burning people alive—resonates with a unique, self-selecting audience of people who are not repelled by such atrocities and may even seek to participate in them. Intensive media coverage of terrorist attacks like those in Brussels, Ottawa, Sydney, Paris, and Copenhagen or of stabbings or driving automobiles into crowds provide further incitement to jihadist fanatics and jihadist loons.

Since the latter part of 2013, the terrorist jihad has been distracted by the schism between the supporters of al-Qaeda and the supporters of the Islamic State. Competition between these groups' leaderships for pledges of loyalty and expressions of support continues. Open warfare between the two factions has occurred in Syria. Victory by one over the other seems unlikely. The jihadist movement will always be subject to centrifugal forces, but the current split may or may not persist.

The internal divisions have not prevented the spread of jihadist ideology and establishment of new jihadist footholds, whether these display al-Qaeda's black standard or the logo of the Islamic State. Beyond Syria and Iraq lies a complex landscape of shifting loyalties.

In addition to AQAP in Yemen and al-Nusra in Syria, al-Qaeda counts on its Somali affiliate, al-Shabaab, and its North African affiliate, al-Qaeda in the Islamic Maghreb (or AQIM), which has some presence in Tunisia. Al Murabitun is a splinter group of AQIM operating in the Sahel. In late 2014, al-Qaeda established a new front in India, calling it al-Qaeda in the Indian Subcontinent, or AQIS.

Ansar al Sharia in Libya and Tunisia (the two are distinct organizations) remain unaffiliated, although some of their members have declared their loyalty to the Islamic State, which has been recruiting from various al-Qaeda and independent groups. An estimated 3,000 Tunisians and over 500 Libyans are reportedly fighting in Syria and Iraq.

Boko Haram in Nigeria and Ansar al Maqdis or Ansar Jerusalem, operating in Egypt's Sinai desert, have both pledged loyalty to the Islamic State, as have some disgruntled Taliban leaders in Afghanistan.

The recent attack on Western tourists in Tunisia and explosions at Shia mosques in Yemen, both of which were claimed by the Islamic State, along with the closing of American diplomatic facilities in Saudi Arabia, underscore the danger posed by the spread of jihadist ideology and radicalizing role of the conflicts in Syria and Iraq.

Despite the poaching of recruits and mustering oaths, in fact, the feud between al-Qaeda and the Islamic State has little relevance outside of the war zone in Syria. Neither side in the internal quarrel exercises direct control over home-grown jihadists, where the push for action comes as much from the bottom as it does from the top. Some Western jihadists even welcome the split, hoping that it will lead to competition between the two wings of the movement to see which can carry out more spectacular attacks in the West.

Both al-Qaeda and ISIL believe that communications are as important as the armed struggle. Both have effectively exploited the internet, al-Qaeda in a more controlled manner and ISIL using social media. We have never really abated the power of the message coming from al-Qaeda, and now ISIL, through its actions and communications, has amplified that message to inspire a broader audience. That message will continue to spread and fuel instability in regional conflicts.

There is, nonetheless, good news—in that neither al-Qaeda nor ISIL has achieved more than limited success in persuading Americans to join their version of jihad. The terrorist organizations have not been able to build a deep reservoir of support here; there have been few terrorist plots, and thus far there is no exodus of U.S. volunteers going to Syria.

The most likely threat to U.S. homeland security therefore comes from home-grown terrorists carrying out unsophisticated, but lethal, attacks. As we have seen in the terrorist assaults at Fort Hood, Paris, and Tunis, or numerous non-terrorist shootings in the United States, a pair of gunmen, or even just one, can cause serious casualties. Over the long term, we cannot exclude the possibility of more ambitious plots, although domestic intelligence efforts have been remarkably successful.

Chairman McCAUL. Thank you, Mr. Jenkins. The Chairman now recognizes myself for questions. I look back—the President's campaign narrative was to end the war in Iraq and Afghanistan and shut down Guantanamo. We were so quick to withdraw out of Iraq, we failed to negotiate a status of forces agreement and the political malfeasance with the Prime Minister Maliki and his purging of the Sunni tribes, those two factors coupled together I think created the formation of ISIS.

I think this President has had a hard time getting his head wrapped around, how could this have happened under my watch? How could ISIS have happened? Now we have seen the establishment of a caliphate in Iraq and Syria and we are also seeing what I call forward operating bases now in northern Africa and throughout the Middle East.

We are seeing the rapid destabilization. We saw that in Yemen. It happened in Libya. We saw Tunisia being hit, and it is all throughout northern Africa, including when we had to shut down our embassies temporarily in Saudi Arabia.

This is alarming to me, and I agree with the Speaker that we are currently losing this war. But I always think the first premise when you fight a war, and it is, is to define the enemy to defeat them. Yet the President fails to call it what it is, and that is radical Islamist extremism.

Mr. Speaker can you tell me why some discount that, that it is just not important? General Hayden, I think you talked about the house of Abraham. I saw the structure of his house in Iraq and the three major religions coming out of that house, I hope one day we can coexist peacefully. It may not happen in my lifetime but I want it to happen in my children's lifetime. But it is theologically-based.

So Mr. Speaker, can you tell me why that is so important?

Mr. GINGRICH. Thank you. I think the core thing to understand here, and this goes way beyond the current administration. This was also true under President Bush. We had a fundamental misunderstanding of our enemies from Day 1. This is a movement. It is not an organization. You can't take Cold War models of the Communist Party structure, just as you can't take Western models of state-to-state conflict.

This movement has been out there. You can argue when it should start. I am actually thinking about trying to put together a course on this. Because you can argue it starts with Khomeini coming back from Paris and issuing his book on Islamic governance. You can argue that it starts with the war in Afghanistan and people like the mujahedin becoming more and more radicalized.

You can argue it starts with the Muslim Brotherhood and the degree to which their leadership right after World War II was deeply offended by the West. I mean, they come in a room like this, they see women sitting here, they know this is sinful, they know this is evil and they say so.

They go back and they say, look, we are being destroyed. When Khomeini said we were the great Satan, he really meant our cultural system was a direct assault on everything he believed in. We don't understand, this is a movement. You know, ISIS didn't exist 2½ years ago. So the focus now on ISIS is just one more example of the American model of bunchball, where we all rush to the latest thing and then we are going to focus on Boko Haram and then we will focus on al-Shabab. The fact is, there is a world-wide movement. It is connected by religious fanaticism. It exists in both a physical and cultural warfare model. None of that is permitable in the current American governing structure. You can't have this conversation in the Executive branch. I think it means we have—and this is not about Obama. We as a country have a huge problem because we can't even describe who opposes us.

Chairman MCCAUL. General Hayden, we pulled our embassy out of Yemen. With that goes a great degree of our intelligence footprint capability, as you know as former director of the CIA, NSA. The special forces now are withdrawing.

AQAP, one of the biggest threats to the United States in terms of external operations, five plots in recent years, including the Christmas day bomber, responsible also for the Paris attacks. These are the ones, when you say who was most likely hit the United States, it is always AQAP. Yet now we are completely withdrawing so they can operate with impunity.

My concern, and quite frankly, sir, given your experience, is the lack of coverage that we are going to have now, lack of ability to know what is going on on the ground and a lack or inability to attack AQAP before they can attack us. Can you comment on that?

General HAYDEN. I can, Mr. Chairman. I can imagine what is going on at Langley now as they try to recover or at least sustain some of the things that had been going on in Yemen. Your question is fundamentally about the physical pressure we were able to maintain on al-Qaeda in the Arabian Peninsula. We had two broad thrusts there I think. One was cooperating with the Yemeni government and using their forces to create that kind of physical pressure. Well, that government no longer exists so that is off the table.

We had our own forces there largely through targeted killings. Targeted killings require exquisite intelligence and there is no secret sauce there. It is fabric that is created out of all varieties and streams of intelligence collection.

So let's look now at what is our capacity to continue targeted killings. Tactical intelligence will continue. I suspect it will be a little degraded but pretty much stays in place. Liaison with the government in Yemen, that is gone.

Then finally, the human sources, which are really critical in making sure you are being very correct when you apply violence with this kind of precision. The human source networks will continue but I suspect they will erode over time because of our lack of physical presence in the country. So I think the overall assessment is the physical pressure we had on al-Qaeda in the Arabian Peninsula is reduced and, barring something like a return, it will continue to erode as we go forward.

Chairman MCCAUL. Thank you, and I would submit it is also true in Libya and in Syria today. I am very concerned about this.

The Chairman recognizes the Ranking Member.

Mr. THOMPSON. Thank you very much. Mr. Speaker, let me say how I appreciate your historical analysis of how we got to where we are today, and the fact that rather than just blame President Obama, you talked about the broader perspective.

General Hayden, let me say how I appreciate you understanding the fact that when a situation is bad that sometimes we have to take our men and women out of a situation, reassess, and come back with a different strategy. All our brave people do a wonderful job, but at some point if situations become intolerable, you have to retreat for an alternate strategy.

So I think my concern is for you, sir, is based on what I have heard from the testimony, it is absolutely imperative that we identify what allies we have left in the region, that we create some kind of a strategy to address this in a broader fashion because their enemy is our enemy and we have to convince our allies that that is what we have to do. Obviously we are going to have to have a significant burden with that task. I understand that.

General, can you tell me if that strategy of working with our allies is still a good strategy going forward?

General HAYDEN. It is, Congressman, and even if it has its failings, in many cases there are few and sometimes no other options available. So we have eroded the cooperation with the Yemeni government now, which has ceased to function. We have very strong relationships with the Saudi government, whose interest in Yemen is at least as strong as ours, and so I am sure that we are deepening the liaison relationship with them as well.

Phil mentioned the importance of liaison in our past successful efforts, but the fact is we are going to have to be very agile. Frankly, and I don't mean to refer to the Saudis in this light, but frankly begin to cooperate with some folks in an ideal world we would rather not have on our side because of the great threat posed by the extremists right now.

One other thing I would mention, Congressman, is on that decision to remove the forces, Special Forces from Yemen, to evacuate the embassy, I feel as if I have no right or grounds to second-guess that decision. That is kind of like the field commander has got to call it as he sees it. People like us, like me just support the field commander making that decision.

Mr. THOMPSON. Mr. Speaker, you want to comment on whether working with allies is still a good strategy in this fight against terrorism?

Mr. GINGRICH. I think working with allies is the only strategy that will work. I mean almost all of our successful wars, whether it is World War II, or the Cold War, we have always tried to surround ourselves with allies.

The fact is, in some cases—I mean it is unfortunate right now that, for example, the administration is not doing more to reinforce el-Sisi, who is the President of Egypt, and who has taken exactly the right position on the need to reform Islamic views to make them more modern.

But I also want to reemphasize something which has been said by several people up here. We are going to have a lot—we are going to have allies that make us uncomfortable. We are going to have allies that don't fit the test of exact purity. Let me just be a little controversial since I used to serve up here.

You know it would be really helpful for the Congress to go to the agencies and find out, what are the things Congress has imposed over the last 40 years that make agility impossible? What are the things Congress has imposed that make working with difficult allies very dangerous?

I mean we have managed to set a standard of purity which cripples us in dealing with this. We have managed to set a standard of bureaucracy, which virtually guarantees we won't be agile. Congress is going to have to reform those things because they are written into the law.

Mr. THOMPSON. Mr. Jenkins, with the time I have left, do you see the lone-wolf scenario as a clear and present danger for us here in this country?

Mr. JENKINS. First of all, I despise the term lone wolf. I just think that it romanticizes and elevates these adversaries. I have always instead used the term stray dogs. That is not to be insulting, but the problem we face is you know you—it is very, very difficult to predict dangerousness.

We have these people that are on the internet. They are barking. They are snapping. They are exhorting each other to action. To try to figure out which one is going to bite is very, very difficult.

I mean and so this is a problem we have. As these volumes of home-grown and foreign fighters increase, that just increases the problem overall.

Thus far we have been really fortunate here in that in the United States, in terms of Americans getting involved in this, we have had a number of dangerous people. But the numbers are nowhere comparable to what we see taking place in Europe. That is the good news.

The second part of the good news is that these plots, many of them have been remarkably amateurish and have been—there is a reason for that. That is because a lot of them are one-offs. These are not terrorist groups that are able to carry on continued operations.

I mean in the 1970s we were dealing with 50 to 60 terrorist bombings a year in this country. But that was carried out by groups, whether on the far left or far right or motivated by foreign quarrels. They carried on those campaigns. They started out as incompetent. Over a period of time they learned how to do it and got better. We don't have that now.

The third piece of good news is that our domestic intelligence, while still not optimal, has been extremely effective in identifying and breaking up a lot of these plots.

So we do face some dangers. But thus far we have been able to contain this at, as I say, a much lower level than we are seeing abroad. That doesn't mean that one—two persons or even one person getting hold of a gun can't be a lethal opponent and carry out an attack that would create alarm and reactions in this country that would go far beyond even the actual casualties.

Mr. THOMPSON. Thank you very much. I yield back.

Chairman MCCAUL. Chairman recognizes Mr. Smith from Texas.

Mr. SMITH. Thank you, Mr. Chairman. I will yield my time to the gentleman from Texas, Mr. Ratcliffe, and happy to have him ask questions.

Mr. RATCLIFFE. Thank the gentleman. I would like to thank the witnesses here for giving testimony today and being willing to discuss what I think is perhaps the most critical topic of our day. I say that as a former U.S. attorney and as a former terrorism prosecutor who has seen and learned first-hand the gravity of the threat that violent Islamic extremism poses to the United States and to the rest of the world.

I have also seen where President Obama has recently declared that al-Qaeda is on the run. He of course has mocked ISIS as the junior varsity. He in fact refuses to use the word Islam and terrorism in the same sentence.

In short, I think that the administration's approach is making our efforts to defend and defeat this threat even more difficult. I think that this is underscored by the fact, and reflected in the fact that we have now been forced to pull out of Syria. We have been forced to pull out of Libya. We have been forced to pull out of Yemen.

So my first question to you, Speaker Gingrich, is: Has the pullout in Syria, Libya, and Yemen compromised, in your opinion, our ability to intercept Islamic terrorist threats as they develop?

Mr. GINGRICH. Well, I would say two things. One—and I would be interested in the comments of other folks up here at this table who have much more professional background in this. I think it is a very different environment than anything we historically analyzed.

Remember, ISIS is actually serving as a magnet to draw thousands of people. I just saw a study of where ISIS tweets come from and the U.S. ranks fourth, far above Pakistan, far above even Jordan. The number of people who are tweeting have been in favor of ISIS.

So you have a very different kind of environment now. I would say that what is happening in part is that you are having—and this by the way, people at the CIA were warning me about as early as December 2001. But what you are having is an attractiveness for people who are alienated and who are looking for some meaning in their life.

So even if you tomorrow morning could crush ISIS part of the result might be that you would send 10,000 foreign fighters back home who would actually spread the virus. We need to think of this as an epidemiology problem. This is not a statecraft problem.

I would say that clearly, I mean the fact that we have closed our embassy in Saudi Arabia out of fear for physical safety should be a wake-up call to everybody in this country. The Saudis are very tough. If they are worried enough that we are closing the embassy, even though temporarily, I think there are things under way that are dangerous.

To not understand we have a two-front war. You have the Iranians who are the leading sponsor of state terrorism, and you have a Sunni-based terrorism. They are both our mortal enemies. They both would be happy to destroy us. We have no strategy for either one right now.

Mr. RATCLIFFE. Thank you, Mr. Speaker.

General Hayden, I would be interested in your insights on the same question.

General HAYDEN. Sure. It is the closure of embassies and consulates both cause and effect here, all right. It is the effect of our losing control of the situation. It is also the cause of our losing control of the situation. As we withdraw and that footprint on the ground goes away, we just have a lower level of knowledge of the situation there.

I would add an additional thought. I will try to use the language of the region. When we go about closing embassies and not having diplomatic presence and so on, we look weak.

The concept of the strong horse and the weak horse is a very important concept in this part of the world. So we appear to be a nation in retreat when we take these kinds of steps, in addition to the concrete operational effects that it has.

Mr. RATCLIFFE. Thank you, general. I would like to ask you another question because in a recent piece that you wrote for the *Washington Times* earlier this month you noted that the administration and its negotiating partners have conceded Iran's right to enrich through this process.

You quoted Henry Kissinger, saying that the administration has decided to ''manage rather than prevent nuclear proliferation.'' My question is simply this: I would like your insight on the broader impact of this nuclear agreement with respect to future—our ability to affect future counter proliferation efforts.

General HAYDEN. I think it has a dark effect on it, Congressman. A couple of things come to mind. No. 1, a struggling, at best, regional power, it would have just stared down the world and six of the most powerful nations on the planet and has now been allowed to have an industrial strength nuclear program. An awful lot of other countries are going to school on that. So I think the effects globally are bad.

The effects locally are bad because I don't think the Sunni states, and the speaker has emphasized this Sunni-Shia split may be becoming the defining flavor of this violence. I don't think the Sunnis will let that stand without a response on their part.

Then finally, when you get this agreement, despite the fact that all the other characteristics of Iran—let's even say it is successful, all right, which might be problematic. All the other defining characteristics of Iranian states, whether of terrorism, regional hegemony, moving into Iraq and so on, all that stays in place. But they are no longer the international outlaw that they once were. With the signing of this agreement they become more or less a normal country, which makes all these other factors even worse.

Mr. RATCLIFFE. Thank you, general.

I have questions for all of the witnesses. I wish I had more time to ask them. I again want to thank you all for being here. This is, again, a vitally important issue. Your testimony is going to be critical in forming our opinions going forward on this committee. Thank you for being here. I will thank the gentlemen again and yield back.

Chairman MCCAUL. Thank you.

The Chairman recognizes Mr. Higgins.

Mr. HIGGINS. Thank you, Mr. Chairman.

General Hayden, particularly in your testimony you talked about the Shia-Sunni divide. The current head of ISIS is Abu Bakr al-Baghdadi.

Abu Bakr al-Baghdadi takes his name from Abu Bakr, who was a companion of the Prophet Muhammad. He was not a prophet himself, but also the father-in-law of the Prophet Muhammad. He was the first caliph in Val Nasser's ''The Shia Revival.''

He talks about the divide between Shia and Sunni in that in certain parts of the Middle East Sunnis believe that Shia are apostates, they are nonbelievers. He also believes that—some believe that Shias have tails.

I just want to deal with what we have today within the historical context of what we know only too well. We were told that there would be an international response to degrade and destroy ISIS. We were told that this coalition would consist of 62 countries, including many of the 22-member Arab League nations. Look at the record. From the air last month General Lloyd Austin said that 8,500 ISIS militants were killed by coalition air strikes in Iraq and Syria.

To date, coalition forces conducted 1,631 airstrikes in Iraq; 1,551 or 70 percent were conducted by the United States. Coalition forces conducted 1,262 airstrikes in Syria; 1,169 or 93 percent were carried out by the United States.

Of the 1,262 coalition airstrikes in Syria, only 84 were conducted by Arab nations of Jordan, Bahrain, Saudi Arabia, and the United Arab Emirates combined. None of the Arab nations are conducting airstrikes in Iraq. Where is the international coalition, including the Arab League?

The United States has also provided $2.9 billion in humanitarian aid to Syria, far more than anybody else. The United States continues to provide record humanitarian and development assistance to Iraq.

Let's move to the ground. The CIA estimates that there are 31,000 ISIS fighters in Iraq and Syria. ISIS controls Iraq's second-largest city of Mosul with between 1,000 and 2,000 fighters embedded there.

Mosul has a population of a million people. We are told that to retake Mosul we need between 20,000 and 25,000 Iraq and Kurdish forces that will be required to clear block-by-block ISIS from Mosul after United States air strikes are conducted there.

United States spent $26 billion to build a 250,000-member Iraqi army. The first test of the Iraqi army was against ISIS last July. The Iraqi army folded, to put it mildly.

Also, there are by some estimates between 400,000 and 800,000 Shia militias supporting the Iraqi army today. The problem is they have a sectarian goal, not a nationalist goal. Those militias are directed by a guy by the name of Qasem Soleimani. Soleimani is the commander of the Quds Force in Iran who is now on the ground in Iraq.

Further, earlier this year the new Prime Minister Abadi announced a major assistance plan for Kurdistan consisting of 17 percent of all Iraq's oil revenues in perpetuity, and $1 billion to support the Kurdish army, the Peshmerga. Peshmerga are an experienced and effective fighting force of some 180,000.

Now we are told that we might need American troops on the ground in addition to the 3,000 that we currently have there. Where is the international coalition? Where is the Arab League?

So, the math just doesn't add up. You got between 400,000 and 800,000 Shia militias supported by our guy in Iraq. You got 180,000 Peshmerga who just did an oil revenue and military support deal with our guy in Iraq.

Then you have the Iraqi army who ran last year from ISIS. Now we are told because of a change in government for a few months they now have the will and the skill to fight ISIS. My concern is this: 1.3 million Iraq fighters should be able to retake Mosul of 1,000 or 2,000 ISIS fighters. They should be able to take on 31,000 estimated ISIS fighters in Iraq and Syria.

Without a clear national agenda, not a sectarian one, we may be looking at deploying American troops into what potentially will be a second civil war, in the same decade, essentially alone again.

See, in that part of the world where there is no political center you only have sides. While the overlay is that the American presence is vitally important to defeat ISIS, and we have demonstrated clearly a willingness to do that and to commit resources to it.

But in that part of the world there is also not only the morning after, but the morning after the morning after. As the Speaker said, you know they are just waiting to get ISIS out of there so they can have their civil war. That is the dilemma that we are dealing with.

I took a lot of time for the question. I apologize for not leaving a lot of time for the answer.

General HAYDEN. Just a couple of comments come to mind, Congressman. First of all, with regard to the American footprint, I don't think anyone responsible is calling for American combat brigades to be maneuvering in the Syrian or Iraqi desert again. But I do think our rules of engagement make our current deployment less effective than it would otherwise be.

We don't allow our forces to go forward below brigade echelon levels, which means that they don't stiffen the local forces. It is more difficult to call in precise tactical airstrikes. We don't have

29

our own reach out and touch people arm with regard to American Special Forces.

With regard to the Peshmerga, they are very large, actually quite good. I actually think they are our best friends in the region. But they have largely been a checkpoint army. They have been responsible for local security. So there is a transition there, not just with training but with equipment.

You mentioned the Sunni-Shia divide. Absolutely. Right now, as I think you suggested, what we have are Shia militias under Iranian officers attempting to retake Tikrit, an overwhelmingly Sunni town. That is not part of the solution. That is a continuation of the problem. I think we should judge it to be that way.

Then finally with boots on the ground, sooner or later we will need boots on the ground. My sense is we are going to have to have Sunni feet in those boots from one country or many from the region. Otherwise it will be for naught.

Chairman MCCAUL. Gentleman's time is expired. Mr. King is recognized.

Mr. KING. Thank you, Mr. Chairman.

Let me thank all the witnesses for their testimony. Speaker, it is always good to see you back.

General Hayden, my first question would be to you. Congressman Ratcliffe mentioned Iran and also the op-ed that you wrote the other day. As I understand the press reports, negotiators are seeking a verification spectrum regime that would keep Iran a year away from enriching enough fissile material to make a bomb.

You stated in the op-ed that the 1-year breakout time may not be sufficient to detect and reverse Iranian violations. Can you expand on that and say why you believe the verification regime may not be sufficient?

General HAYDEN. Yes, sir. First of all, a year looks like a long period of time and from some aspects it is.

I co-authored that with Olli Heinonen from the IAEA. So Olli brought his knowledge of how things work in Vienna. I brought my background with how things work in the American intelligence community.

We gamed it out. We didn't take a long time before we began to figure out scenarios in which it would be very difficult to mobilize action within a 12-month period.

First of all, Mr. Chairman, you have got the distance between flash and bang. You have got from the Iranian violation to the first detection of the Iranian violation, which may be a considerable period of time. You go from the first detection to building up a body of evidence that you can convince the American Government that what you have got here is a very serious problem.

I can only imagine, Congressman, what the burden of proof is going to look like if whether director of National intelligence goes into the Oval Office and says, Mr. President we have got a real issue here.

After the President has decided that we have got a real issue here, he has got to take it to the international community because, as you well know, as this thing is rolling out it is going to be the Security Council that is going to validate this agreement.

So to un-validate this agreement will require us going first to Vienna to get the international inspectors to look at that which we suspect. Then from Vienna to New York in order to aggregate international action to give us sanction to take whatever steps we think might be necessary.

You go to New York you are trying to convince the Russians and the Chinese. So it is not hard to imagine scenarios in which a year isn't enough to mobilize action that would truly deter the Iranians from completing the break-out.

Mr. KING. Thank you, general. Let me also—I would be remiss if I didn't thank you for the—all the free advice and counsel you have given me over the years. So thank you very much. Let me ask—I guess starting with Newt and going across. It has been mentioned that General Sisi has really stepped forward as a moderate Muslim speaking to secular-type interpretation. If each of the four of you can comment on the fact that we are denying weapons systems right now to President Sisi. Any of you? Newt? Mr. Speaker, excuse me.

Mr. GINGRICH. I think this administration is almost 180 degrees off in reality about what is going on in Egypt. The Muslim Brotherhood is our enemy, not our friend. Yet the State Department meets with the Muslim Brotherhood.

El-Sisi, who may not represent everything you would like in good government, does represent a very long Egyptian tradition that has been very hostile to radical Islamists, and is very much desirous of being an ally of the United States. I think we should be doing everything we can to strengthen him and to reinforce his legitimacy.

Because as General Hayden said, you would like him to look like the strong horse, not the weak horse. You would like people to think gee, if you are an ally of the United States the world gets better, it doesn't get worse. The administration is almost precisely opposite what it should be in reality.

General HAYDEN. I would add to that very briefly, look, I was made uncomfortable by what the general did in the year or so after he took power from Mohamed Morsi. There are too many people in jail and there are too many journalists in jail.

But all that said, we talked about, you know, we don't get to pick all of our partners in this war, despite discomfort with some of the things he has done, he is going to be one of the more acceptable partners in this conflict.

I see every advantage in our repairing our relationship with him.

Mr. KING. Mr. Mudd.

Mr. MUDD. If you look at some of the successes in recent years, it is groups of governments, I am thinking of the African Union in Somalia. I think the Nigerians will have a lot of success against Boko with Cameroon, Mali, et cetera.

I think Sisi has the opportunity, when you are looking at a place like Libya, to give us a local partner so that we don't have to either wait for nothing to happen or intervene ourselves.

That said, let's talk about a very simple choice. When you have the transition after the Arab revolutions, you have the choice between elections that lead to Islamists who cause problems, and support for authoritarian regimes that will fight Islamists and favor U.S. interests, but will not lead to one man-one vote.

So do you want security or do you want democracy? They are not mixing well after the 2011 revolutions.

Mr. KING. You mentioned Libya, should we have given Egypt more support when they took action in Libya? Mr. Mudd.

Mr. MUDD. I think so. Again, I am just a practitioner who looks at where we succeed. There are some questions about the fact that there was a lack of Arab support despite the sort of papering over of what is going on in Iraq, in other words, not a lot of Arab action there.

I think the Egyptians have a lot of options for us in Libya. I would suggest if we do that we bring in some other players so it is not just us and Egypt.

Mr. KING. Mr. Jenkins.

Mr. JENKINS. I think you have to put the events in Iran and the events in Egypt together. On the one hand, as Iran edges closer to acquisition of a nuclear weapon, or the perception that it is about to have one, that is—that gives them three things.

It is a scepter of power. It is a potential deterrent that makes going against them in the future more difficult. But more importantly, it emboldens a more aggressive policy of backing subversion because they think they now have protection and can get away with it.

At the same time, if you look at our relationship with Egypt, we have demonstrated a degree of unreliability, not to say fecklessness in terms of there.

Those two things affect everyone's calculations in the region. These are practical people. Apart from the ideology-driven people, these are practical people who say, all right, the Americans want us to do this, they want intelligence, they want troops, they want us to participate in their coalition.

Now if we get in a jam, are the Americans going to be a reliable partner that will back us up? Or are we going to get lectures about democracy and other issues, which are not unimportant to us, but, as I say, they are going to make those kind of cold-blooded calculations because they have to survive in a very rough neighborhood.

Mr. KING. Thank you very much.

I yield back, Mr. Chairman, thank you.

Chairman MCCAUL. The Chairman recognizes the gentlelady from New York, Miss Rice.

Miss RICE. Thank you, Mr. Chairman.

General Hayden, you are the most experienced military tactician on this panel. You are the primary decision maker regarding America's strategy to combat violent Islamist extremism.

Now putting aside the politics of how we got here, and in the interest of coming up with real solutions, can you lay out in detail what your game plan would be?

General HAYDEN. Well, that is a tall order, ma'am. But a couple of——

Miss RICE. I have every confidence you can handle it.

[Laughter.]

General HAYDEN. A couple of high points: Let's look at ISIS as kind of a close-in problem. I frankly think that our strategy with regard to ISIS in Iraq is coherent. I think it is under-resourced, all right. I don't think we are leaning forward enough. We talked about rules of engagement, what we allow our forces to do.

So there I would double-down. I would particularly double-down on the Kurds as a reliable partner.

I don't see coherence yet in our strategy with regard to ISIS in Syria. We are keeping their heads down. We are rooting their capacity. We are making them less rich than they used to be, therefore less capable.

But I don't think anything we are doing yet there in anyway fits into the decisive column. So there I think we need to do some heavier lifting, forces on the ground so that we actually have kind of a hammer and anvil with air power and ground forces.

I would also reinvestigate why it is we keep the regime off the table in terms of people we include to be our enemy there.

So that is with regard to ISIS. We also have kinetic activity we have talked about in Somalia, in Yemen, again, degrading those folks who are already convinced they want to come kill us.

Ma'am, the most serious problem I see is the production rate of people who want to come kill us in 3, 5, or 10 years. That gets back to the ideological issue that we have talked about here.

There, it is a tough game. I can't—we were actually very successful in the Bush administration with the close-in fight, those folks already committed to come and kill us. We were not nearly as successful with the deep fight, the ideological fight. That still remains the one we have to do.

A very quick anecdote. I was President Obama's CIA chief for 3 weeks. During one of those weeks we actually achieved an operational act in the CIA that made America safer.

Rahm Emanuel came up and said, good on you, that is really good stuff. I had the temerity to say to the President's chief of staff, thank you very much, that is very kind, but you understand, if we don't change the facts on the ground, we get to do this forever.

We have to defend ourselves now, protect ourselves, buy time, but then we have got to make use of that time on these broader strategic issues.

Miss RICE. Thank you, General.

Mr. Jenkins, what is a greater threat to the United States, the radicalization of Americans at home or the threat of foreign fighters returning to the United States after becoming radicalized in another country?

Mr. JENKINS. I am not recognized in the field of prophecy, so I am not going to try to say which would—both of them are simply different dimensions of the threat. As I said, thus far despite an intensive campaign, at least by al-Qaeda, now this is changing with the Islamic State.

But at least by al-Qaeda, they have made an intensive on-line sales campaign. They haven't sold a lot of cars. That is good news.

The Islamic State is different in that they have been—whereas al-Qaeda's communications were much more centrally directed and controlled through websites that favored them.

ISIS has made much greater use of social media, and therefore it has reached a larger and younger audience who live in that media environment, and has had a greater effect.

The real question here in the long run is, is that going to really change enough of them or is this becoming kind of a conveyor for youthful discontents and rebellion? I don't know about 15-year-old girls from Colorado running off to some romance with the desert version of Hannibal Lecter.

I mean, but——

Miss RICE. Well, why have they been more effective with their messaging and their wooing of non-Americans rather than Americans? Is the message different? Is the—what is——

Mr. JENKINS. It is interesting, when you look at the individual biographies, they say where they are getting their big numbers is out of Europe. There is no question there that there are large unassimilated, marginalized immigrant diasporas, whereas in the American community where certainly we are a nation of immigrants as well, but we have been, and this is good news for us, again, much more successful in assimilating these people.

So if you look at the—at, for example, education levels of the Americans who are being wooed into this, it is roughly the equivalent of the same age educational level of the general population.

What you find instead therefore you find much more individual motives, someone feels their "life sucks": That is a quote. They are—they feel insulted. There is—no question, however uncomfortable that makes us, there is an element of religious motivation in this. But it is added to senses of anger, alienation, desire to do something meaningful, participate in an epic adventure. If you, in contrast, go to some of these other places where they are picking up a lot of people, there you really see a—much more of a community-based issue as opposed to an individual-based issue.

Now, as I say, with the ability through social media to reach a much broader audience of young people, are they going—is that going to remain virtual? I mean, as I said, al-Qaeda has created an on-line virtual army; fortunately, it remains mostly virtual.

Is ISIS going to get smarter at this and be able to actually generate something beyond a lot of people tweeting and doing other things? I am not sure. So far they are picking up more people who intend or try to travel to Syria and Iraq.

So they are getting a bigger purchase on an audience than we have seen before. That is a long-term concern.

Chairman MCCAUL. The gentlelady's time has expired.

Miss RICE. Thank you, Mr. Chairman.

Chairman MCCAUL. The Chairman now recognizes Mr. Perry.

Mr. PERRY. Thank you, Mr. Chairman.

Gentlemen, thank you for your service.

I will start with Mr. Mudd, if you could. Would you be able to rate the current administration regarding home-grown terrorism, radicalization here at home, and the things that we have done to combat it or to deal with it in the macro and the micro sense?

Assuming that you might have a divergent opinion, can you contrast what would you do differently from what is currently being done, if you can, on a macro sense, anyhow?

Mr. MUDD. Let me give you a few thoughts. I did serve on loan from the CIA to the FBI for about 4½ years, so I watched this from the inside. Operationally I think we do pretty well. If you look at what we anticipated 14 years ago, we got a lot less than we anticipated. When you are at the threat table in 2001, 2002, and 2003 and somebody tells you we will not suffer a catastrophic event in this country, you would have said, no way. We did not understand the adversary.

In terms, and so, we could talk about operationally, but I think the Bureau uses a lot of resources. I don't think it is particularly efficient. That is not a criticism. It is just because they are charged by people like you to make sure nothing happens in this country. So we chased everybody we could find with the resources we had when I was in the Bureau.

Ideologically, in terms of this fight on the internet, et cetera, I don't think—this is not a comment on this White House or the other. I am a practitioner and a servant. I am not a politician. I don't think we do very well in this sphere because we want to own it within Government.

I mentioned it earlier when I started speaking, I think there is an opportunity to talk to the people who do own it. For example, I don't want to get into specific companies, but I have talked to some of the companies in this space, that is the social media space. They don't really understand what the adversary looks like. Therefore, they can't offer in my judgment good guidance about how to chase the adversary.

I think they see the U.S. Government as telling them what to do when we want their data, as opposed to saying here is what the target looks like. California, Silicon Valley, can you tell us how you want us to change the law so you can give us data to hunt these folks? I don't think we enable them to get out there and message.

So I don't think the U.S. Government generally and the American system is very good at being agile and influencing the way people think about Islamist ideology. I don't think we should be that good. I think there are other people who would be better. I would suggest that we ask, that we give them what we are facing. I don't think you have to go into a secret environment to do that. I could brief them today.

We tell them that this is what we are facing in the digital world, Facebook, Yahoo, PayPal, all these guys. What would you suggest we do? Let's talk about ideas before you get into legislative changes.

Mr. PERRY. Thank you. Mr. Speaker, I have been a combatant commander and I guarantee you that my troops knew what the mission was and knew who the enemy was, and your testimony particularly centered around the inability, the unwillingness to identify the enemy. It doesn't just stay at the top. It cascades down through the disparate organizations. I am assuming you mean DHS as well.

So with your experience in Government and the whole-of-Government, what do you think that this committee can do to motivate, so to speak, DHS to identify the enemy? I mean, we can't force them to do it. Then craft a policy regarding the identification and the defeat of the enemy within the country, if you would. What could this committee do?

Mr. GINGRICH. Well, first of all, the Congress actually could force a great deal. Now whether or not you get it signed into law in the short run. But if you go back, the last time we faced the kind of penetration we have now was in the 1930s and 1940s with the Soviets, and the Congress was very active in beginning to figure out what was going on and it was very tumultuous. People didn't like it.

You have got to confront the fact that what you now have is a willful denial of objective reality. Well, the Congress does have an ability to pass laws, to make regulations, and then to hold the kind of hearings and investigations to get this stuff out in the open. So I would start there. I would also say, since you have been a combatant commander, one of the things that came up earlier: It bothers me that we have had almost no serious review of what hasn't worked. We have been at this now with thousands of dead, tens of thousands of wounded. We have tried to train armies, which have collapsed. We clearly don't have the correct doctrine for what we are doing, and yet you are not going to go out and find very many people who want to peel back the cloth and figure out what we are doing.

Finally, in terms of winning the ideological war, at its peak under Reagan, the U.S. Information Agency was separate from the State Department and 35 percent the size of State. It was an enormous project, consciously sending out messages that broke the morale of the Soviet empire. We have nothing comparable to that today.

So there are a number of steps you could take, but I think if you simply start by saying you would like to have hearings on, you would like to have your staff investigating, what are new trainees told at DHS? What do the documents look like? What kind of people are brought in to the do the briefings? How are they vetted? I think you will be stunned how methodically and systematically we have become blind over the last 10 or 12 years, and how cultural jihad is more dangerous than physical jihad.

Until we confront that—and you can confront it in this committee by holding hearings about that agency, how it operates, what it tells itself, how it communicates, and you will begin to find out that a great deal of what we currently do is nonsense.

Chairman McCAUL. The Chairman recognizes Mr. Keating.

Mr. KEATING. Thank you, Mr. Chairman. I believe that indeed if you are going to analyze ISIS, ISIL, Daesh, whatever you want to use for a term, there is something to be said clearly that there are those that are true ideologues, people that have this apocalyptic view of things. But I have been talking to people on the ground over there, including military people as well, and they say you can't simplify it that way, that there are different factions.

Now I know, you know, in my own opinion, for instance in the Boston bombing, Tamerlan Tsarnaev, I would say he is more categorized as his uncle called him, a loser, a misfit. You have these people, many of them foreign, you know, some of the foreign fighters that go over there. But there are people that have nothing going on in their life. They have no hope. They are not powerful in their own right. Nothing going on even in the more personal aspects of their life. They are people attracted to the adventure.

Then you have another group I think, that sits sort-of back, the old Baathists and people that lost their power in Iraq, who kind-of want to sit back and influence things as best they can as well.

Another group that has been a faction of this that has been talked about is just the pure criminals there, just out for the money.

So I understand that many of you said that there is a danger in underestimating the ideological part of this, the religious part of this. But I think there is a danger too, to make one size fits all and not look at the other factions that are represented by that and by the things I just mentioned.

Can you comment on that? I mean, if our approach is just one dimensional, there is about four factions I just named, how best are we approaching this? Take your pick.

Mr. GINGRICH. Who would you like——

Mr. KEATING. Well, I was hoping there would be a little leadership in answering that question.

[Laughter.]

Mr. GINGRICH. Let me just say as a historian, you could have made exactly the same argument about the Communists and exactly the same argument about the Nazis. The Nazis gained an enormous amount of their power by attracting every loser in Germany and giving them a sense of meaning. The communists used some of the dumbest people on the planet.

But the core operating model in both cases was highly ideological and was led by people quite prepared to die for what they believed in. All the evidence we have so far is that these—and I emphasize, it is a movement. I think we waste far too much energy arguing over organizational structures. There is a world-wide movement that is gaining momentum that is best dealt with as an epidemiology problem. The core momentum there is clearly driven by a sense of religious imperative.

Mr. KEATING. My impression, and I did a little work on this, a good example because it is my home State, is Tamerlan Tsarnaev is no ideologue. He is a loser. He was. So I don't think that holds for all the people being attracted to this. They are attracted for different reasons, and part of it will deal with how the misgovernance in a lot of these areas and the corruption continues to create problems.

Again, if we are one-dimensional, just ask any of the other three, do you think it is that simple? It is just one group and you're just going to ignore all the other factions?

General HAYDEN. Let me revisit something I just suggested in my opening comments, that indeed an awful lot of recruiting looks more like why young Americans join the Crips and the Bloods than it has to do with the holy Quoran. I understand that. It is alienation, it is something bigger than self and so on.

But it also matters, I think as the Speaker suggested, it also matters what gang you join. This particular gang at the top is driven by this messianic, apocalyptic vision, which then makes these misfits joining that organization more dangerous than other——

Mr. KEATING. Well, I just suggest this, that that is good in part, in my opinion, and I don't disagree at all. Let's wipe out the leadership of this group. Let's get Baghdadi, let's get all of them. But if we don't deal with those other issues I am talking about, there is just going to be a new group coming up. That is the problem we have too.

So if we don't understand that we have to do something with the Sunnis, they have to feel politically connected at all in this and have a place to live, if we don't deal with all these other issues and just spend too much of our time, inordinately so, I think, giving very simple answers, saying, well, the President doesn't recognize who it is, and if we don't call them by name then we can't deal with them. That might sound good in a sound clip, but I am talking about what is really happening.

Don't you think that if we don't deal with all these other issues we are just going to be right back in the same cycle? Because all these other things are just going to bring another leader, another group, another ideological group.

Mr. MUDD. One quick comment on watching the evolution of how these guys think. I think there is a change in evolution about 10 years ago. The first guys we took down at the agency were ideologues. The architects of 9/11 were steeped in thinking about how you could change Islam to justify what they called attacks against the far enemy, the far enemy being the United States.

Overseas and in the United States, I believe starting at about roughly 2005, 2006, we started seeing more emotional motivation, people who would see a photo out of Iraq of a dead baby or a dead woman, saying I have got to go fight the crusaders because I saw this picture on Jazeera. I talked to some of these people. This is not a theory. This is sitting down, why did you go? I saw a photo.

So there is a distinction between an upper echelon-idealogue—they have to die; they are not going to turn back again. The masses who are motivated they think by idealogy, but by emotion.

One closing word. When you think about not how we see this intellectually, but how we talk about this, be careful. The reason is the adversary wants to create this into us versus them. They want to say we are here to protect you in Iraq against the crusaders.

There is now ISIS moving into Afghanistan. You just see interviews from the past couple days of people saying in Afghanistan I want to go fight the crusader in Iraq. The adversary cannot explain to these emotional fellow travelers why murder of innocence is acceptable.

So you can categorize this for this that 98 percent is a fight between good and evil, which is what they want. Or you can categorize it as a fight against people who choose to murder for a political purpose——

Mr. KEATING. My time is up, but I am in agreement with what you said there. But just my point is it is more complex than that.

I yield back.

Chairman MCCAUL. Chairman recognizes Mr. Hurd.

Mr. HURD. Thank you, Mr. Chairman.

Gentlemen, thank you all for being here. It is great to see former colleagues from my days at the CIA. My first question is to General Hayden and Mr. Mudd. You know in December 2001 the fall of Kandahar killed 30 percent of al-Qaeda leadership.

The fall, the Taliban was pushed out of Pakistan. There were 400 Americans on the ground, 100 CIA officers, 300 Special Forces. Is this a model? Or I guess my question is, is that—what are the pros and cons of that model being used in places like Yemen, Syria, Africa? Is that something that can still be done?

Mr. MUDD. Three categories of stuff because I don't think there is one shoe fits all. In certain cases you have a government that is so good at what they do that modest levels of American support. I would think Indonesia. Indonesians have done a great job against what I thought was a significant threat in 2003 Bali attacks, et cetera.

Southern Philippines again, modest American support. That has gone pretty well. Other places you have a constellation of governments that can help. The African Union in Somalia has done well.

I think I mentioned earlier that we can do the same thing with the Nigerians, Somali, Cameroon in Africa. So that is why I was saying support to Sisi might work. I would suggest we figure out if there is a group of people that sort-of spread the pain.

Then finally, and I think we have talked about Iraq a lot. But there are certain countries that there isn't going to be a constellation of power. There is an American interest. There is a major amount of support that is required that we have to go in and say that regardless of whether it says in the newspapers that there is a coalition there is not. The Americans have to get more aggressive if they want to turn back this adversary.

So I would say it depends on how much government you have. It depends on whether that government has a major problem or a modest problem. It depends on whether you can find partners to work. So figure out what the threat is. Figure out what the government capability is locally and work from there.

General HAYDEN. I would agree totally. As you know, we spend an awful lot of time at the agency with what we call liaison. We do it not because we are charitable. We do it because it works. Obviously you can't get out of the liaison service something that they have not put in. But there is generally always something there from which you can benefit.

Mr. MUDD. I am sorry. One more comment. We haven't talked about this enough. Americans are squeamish about this. Drones.

As a practitioner I can tell you there should be a National conversation at some point about where drones are used in environments where we are not at war. For example, is Boko Haram an appropriate target?

My reason is quite simple. If you look at the fundamental characteristics that drive success, in my judgment, for terrorist organizations, its visionary leadership that had the safe haven and time to plot. That used to be Yemen, Somalia, northern Nigeria, Afghanistan. Every single one of these has these characteristics of visionary leadership and safe haven.

When the adversary talks about what brings them pain, and I use this as a litmus test, if they complain about something incessantly, that is a good thing. They hate drones.

So we can be squeamish about talking about the use of lethal force outside war zones. We can be worried, appropriately, about intervening too early and alienating people. But if you want to take out the kinds of leadership who have the vision to say the far enemy in Washington is our enemy, drones have been incredibly effective.

General HAYDEN. Could I just add after you and I said goodbye to one another in Texas yesterday I actually read the documents from the Osama bin Laden cache that were made public in the recent court case in New York.

It is remarkable prose about how painful the targeted killing program was against the al-Qaeda leadership. It is something that I would recommend all of you have your staffs pull some quotes for you to read because Phil is right, it really, really hurt them.

Mr. HURD. Thank you, gentlemen.

My next question is for Mr. Speaker. You talk about the cultural jihad. You know the CIA has traditionally had the role of covert action. In finding al-Qaeda in the late 2000s it was countering— it was propping up moderate imams to counter that threat. You know this is too big. The ISIS's use of social media is too big.

How can the Federal—where should the Federal Government be? How can we be—I know you mentioned you know the U.S. Information Agency during the Communist era. I agree with Mr. Mudd that you know we have to get our partner nations involved in this fight. How do we do that from a Government perspective?

Mr. GINGRICH. I think it is a very important question. I would say first of all, Congress ought to explore reestablishing the USIA as an independent agency. I think we put it in State when I was speaker. I think in retrospect that is a mistake. You need a forward-looking, independent voice that is out there communicating your message.

Second, and this will be very controversial and very hard to do. If we had had today's rules in Italy and France during the elections after World War II, both countries would have gone Communist. It is a fact that we went in very covertly with huge resources to make sure they did not go Communist.

You start with el-Sisi. We should be taking his speech at the university, which is exactly the message we want. That speech should be everywhere in the Muslim world with our help getting it there, and translating it out of Arabic into every local population. So take that example.

I think second, we are going to have to—and this goes back to homeland security. We have both an offensive and a defensive tool here. On offense we want to be communicating our messages on our terms. We want to do it better than our opposition, which today is not true. Ironically, ISIS is better at tweeting than the United States Government.

Second, we defensively want to crush their capacity to communicate. That is going to require some very serious arguments inside the United States about what is and is not legitimate conversation, if we are serious about eliminating the cultural threat as well as the physical threat.

Mr. HURD. Thank you, Mr. Chairman.

Chairman MCCAUL. Chairman now recognizes Mrs. Watson Coleman.

Mrs. WATSON COLEMAN. Thank you, Mr. Chairman. I would like to yield to the gentlelady from Texas.

Ms. JACKSON LEE. I thank the gentlelady, and I think the gentlelady is allowing me to go in front of her and not yielding her time for her time to be able to ask questions. Let me thank you for your courtesies, Congresswoman Watson Coleman. Let me thank the Chairman and the Ranking Member for this very astute and important hearing.

My first remarks are to thank all of you for your service to the country. The Speaker has been the Speaker for a number of us who have had the privilege of serving here in the United States Congress. Certainly, General Hayden, we are aware of your wonderful leadership and service to this Nation. Mr. Mudd and Mr. Jenkins, we cannot do without experts.

My first point is that I think that we must be very clear in Homeland Security and the other committees that terrorism and the fight against terrorism is not a Republican or a Democratic, if you will, singular and sole opportunity to claim service to the country.

I am very grateful for Speaker Gingrich's comments, which many of us have said is that it is vital that the United States, if I may take your words, Congress undertakes a thorough, no-holds-barred review of the long global war in which we are now engaged. Speaker uses radical Islamists. I would use radical Sunnis, radical Shiites encountering extremism.

He is absolutely right that we have to include Intelligence, Armed Services, Foreign Affairs, Judiciary, and Homeland Security and the leadership of the Congress to understand the vital roles these committees play in the securing of the Nation but in the coordination of their work.

I might also say that for a long period of time that I have had the privilege of serving on this committee I have started using the term franchise terrorism. Now we have got lone wolves and a number of other comments.

Let me just say this to General Hayden, if I might. Having been to Yemen and walked the streets when it was in a different status, meeting with leaders, riding in taxicabs, do you think it was appropriate for the administration to remove those Special Forces based upon what I would assume is the intelligence that they had at this point in time? It does not say whether they will return or not return? We have not made that conclusion. But to remove them out of harm's way.

General HAYDEN. Congresswoman, I completely defer to the local commander and the administration. That is not something that should be second guessed. People who are responsible for the safety of our men and women have to make that decision and we should all just live with their judgment.

Ms. JACKSON LEE. I appreciate that because I want to make it very clear that we cannot be successful if we begin to say it is the President's fault, it is this administration's fault. I think Speaker Gingrich nailed it on the head. I may disagree with my colleagues here in Congress, but we have a responsibility to engage in this process.

But I will not sit at this committee table and yield to conversation that suggests that the administration, in this instance President Barack Obama, has in any way failed any more than I am sure there will be challenges to my disagreement with the Iraq War.

My point that the Iraq War left us in a—not in the able wonderful service of our many men and women of whom I visited in Iraq certainly could not stand in their shoes. But did not come to where we wanted it to be primarily because of the very poor leadership of Maliki and what he did with the Shiites and Sunnis.

So let me, quickly, get as I remain here I want to make sure that we stay on the fact that we must be unified. So to both Speaker Gingrich, let me say that I celebrate what you said about the U.S. Information Agency. That is a hot point that we should move on quickly.

So the question is to Mr. Gingrich, Mr. Hayden, and Mr. Jenkins. What are the next steps? We have lone wolves. We have franchise terrorism. We have gangs.

ISIS is the most heinous organization that I think in the history of the United States confronting an international position. We cannot say that it is not. So we cannot condemn a President who other Presidents may have had situations of war, but did not have situations of ISIS.

I would welcome the comments of Speaker Gingrich, General Hayden, and Mr. Jenkins, if you will, and Mr. Mudd, if you don't mind, I am a few seconds from ending.

I thank my colleagues. I thank you very much.

Mr. GINGRICH. Well, let me, first of all, thank the gentlelady for her comments. I think we are in agreement that this should be dealt with as a National issue, not a partisan issue.

We should be dealing with also recognizing that the next President and probably the President after that are gonna be dealing with this. This is a long, difficult process. I said on 9/14 or 9/15, this was a 50- to 75-year war. Since I think we have been off-track for 15 years, unfortunately it is still a 50- to 75-year war.

I would say the first thing Congress could do—this will sound amorphous, but it is really important—the first thing that Congress has to have is a genuine debate about what the war is about. I mean, the Congress has got to decide, is this in fact, as I suggest, an epidemiology that involves a movement, that 15-year-old girls aren't being recruited in Denver accidentally, and that we are up against a world-wide, global campaign, which is gonna force us to change some of our rules and change some of our institutions.

If that is true, then let me repeat the rather bold thing I suggested earlier, which is that Congress ought to ask the National security institutions what are the things that Congress has done over the last 30 years that hamstrings their ability to be effective.

I mean, the amount of junk we have imposed on these agencies and on these departments that makes it impossible for them to have the effectiveness of the Americans between 1941 and 1955.

If you look at the gap in legal requirements, reporting, et cetera, and you will find that we have crippled ourselves and that this institution, the Congress, is as much at the heart of that as anybody else.

I would start with: What is the nature of the war? Actually figure out, with a genuine National debate and resolution to that effect.

Second, a genuine, serious review of what we do to make it impossible for the Executive branch to be effective.

General HAYDEN. Congresswoman, this may reflect my personal experience, a little bit, but, building off of what the Speaker just said, I think it is the power of political consensus here.

It is the volume of American activity, it is the consistency of American activity. So, if we can get the two political branches agreed upon objectives, the strategy and, frankly, what creates the left- and right-hand boundaries of acceptable pursuit of those objectives, I think that goes a long way to solving some of the problems that the Speaker defined.

Ms. JACKSON LEE. Thank you.

Mr. JENKINS. I will just quickly underscore the points made by the Speaker and General Hayden.

Look, World War II and the Cold War were easier, because they were perceived as existential threats, and that did not eliminate debate about strategy, but it imposed a political unity and a unity of effort that lasted over a period of decades, in the case of the Cold War.

We do not have that now. Absent the perception, that perception which focuses our minds, then all sorts of other agendas begin to interfere with this and interfere with what we are doing and why we are doing it.

So, let me go back to the Speaker's advice, in that we really say, what are our National interests in this part of the world? What are our concerns? What is it that we ought to be doing about it? Have we imposed upon ourselves constraints that don't make sense? Which of those constraints, despite the risk that they impose, are we going to take because they are fundamental reflections of American values? When we get that, then within that, certainly there can be political debate, but there cannot be a kind of zigzag course and the lack of unity that weakens us as a country.

Chairman MCCAUL. The gentlelady's time has expired.

Ms. JACKSON LEE. I thank the Chairman and the Ranking Member.

Chairman MCCAUL. The Chairman recognizes Mr. Carter.

Mr. CARTER. Thank you, Mr. Chairman.

Thank all of you for being here. This is, as you can imagine, quite enlightening.

I have to—following from the Congresswoman's recent comments, I am a little bit concerned. I mean, I hear you telling me that President Sisi in Egypt is the type of leader, although he is not perfect, and not everything we want, that we ought to rally around. Then I hear that we are not doing that, that the administration is not doing that.

I am not trying to point fingers here, but I am wondering, the administration is not backing someone who you all agree that this is what we ought to be doing, or at least seem to be agreeing on that.

Then I look at other things that have happened, like Boko Haram, and now they are affiliated with ISIS. Yet, the administration, again, never recognized them as a terrorist threat. It seems to me that the administration is taking the dental theory of ignore your teeth, and they will go away.

I mean, we are ignoring these groups, and they are not going away. I am just wondering, can you prove me wrong? Can you enlighten me and tell me that that is not what is happening?

Mr. Speaker.

Mr. GINGRICH. Well, let me draw a distinction. I do believe that the President and his immediate team have a world view which led them to believe before they came into office that certain strategies would work, and that those strategies involved a dramatic reduction in American forces and it involved a conscious, psychological appeasement of Islam in general, in the hopes that that would reduce the boiling point, if you will, of the problems.

They have followed that strategy. They believe that the Muslim Brotherhood is a reasonable organization, at a time, by the way, when the Saudis have condemned it. The Egyptians have condemned it. The Jordanians have condemned it. When there is a mortal struggle under way between traditional elites and the Muslim Brotherhood, which is at least as vicious as the struggle with al-Qaeda and ISIS, a point that General Hayden has made, that this is a multi-way fight.

I don't have any idea how one changes the President's view. The President—let me be quite clear, as an Army brat, a hard-line Republican obviously tried to beat him twice. The American people picked him to be President. He gets 2 more years of this.

The most we can do is try to surround him with law and try to surround him with appropriations that maximize moving towards a much more effective war footing than we are right now.

But I don't think that—we can't sit around and wait for 2 years. Frankly, just yelling at him doesn't do much good.

Mr. CARTER. Okay. I acknowledge that. I accept that.

Tell me what we can do. Now, you—I mean, General, what can Congress do? What can we——

Mr. GINGRICH. Now, look, let me just start with this. Congress can do investigations and Congress can hold hearings, not just anti-administration investigations, but just trying to surface reality.

Congress can also ask the great departments that are out there of people who have devoted their lifetime to serve this country. That is why I think you go to them and say, tell me what we do to screw up your life, you will be shocked how much information they are gonna give you, because nobody has ever asked them how they could be more effective if they weren't crippled by what is literally 40 years of law and regulation that now lays over their capabilities.

Mr. CARTER. Can you give me an example of a law or regulation that we can do away with that might help?

Mr. GINGRICH. I am yielding to——

Mr. CARTER. Sure.

General HAYDEN. Well, all of us have pointed out that some of our partners in this enterprise will be partners of necessity more or less than partners of choice. That brings up—that is why I mentioned to Congresswoman Jackson Lee, you got to let us know the left- and right-hand boundaries of acceptable behavior here. Because the last thing you want is an agency—or the permanent government is how I would really describe it—going out and doing things about which they believe there is a political consensus. As soon as they have made everyone feel a lot more comfortable and a lot more safe, then be accused of coloring outside those left- and right-hand boundaries.

Again, reflecting my personal history, Congressman, perhaps more than others—you know, Phil is included in this, as well—how much energy did my own agency out at Langley put in over the last 3 years because of the demand to revisit what the agency did with al-Qaeda detainees? Now, that is a tremendous consumption of energy and talent. Believe me, the best of the agency was put on the process because of the nature of the problem.

So, again, that constant political consensus, clear guidance that maybe looking a lot more through the windscreen than through the rearview mirror.

Mr. CARTER. One final question—let me ask you this—how much of a game plan, if you will, would it be for us to try to try to rally around a group there who could fight these people from within? I mean, would that not behoove us as a Nation? But yet, we don't seem to be doing that if we are not rallying around President Sisi.

Mr. JENKINS. You could make a—the United States could, if it decided to, make a major investment to create a counterforce in the region. I am talking about within Syria and Iraq. It would be necessarily a Sunni force. We are not going to get Alawites under Assad or Shias being commanded by Iranian commanders to join it.

Currently, we are talking about training a 5,000-person force. Quite frankly, a 5,000-person force is not going to be a contender in this. It is not even going to be a bit player. Maybe you do it because it is a way of keeping your hand in. Maybe you do it because of political pressure. But if we wanted to, we could say, ''Look, we are going to create a—or try to create a counterforce here, and it is going to represent the Sunnis.''

Now, you can do that; there are questions about how effective it would be militarily. We can probably address that. But as you do that, it is always going to have political consequences. The political consequences are going to be, you are now going to have a—if we are successful, a tough Sunni force that is going to have something to say about its future in Syria and Iraq. That may not be consistent with what current U.S. policy is on Syria and Iraq. But we could do it.

Chairman MCCAUL. The gentleman's time is expired.

The Chairman recognizes Mrs. Watson Coleman.

Mrs. WATSON COLEMAN. Thank you very much, Mr. Chairman. Thank you to each and every one of you for your testimony.

Speaker Gingrich, I appreciate a couple of things that you said—a lot of things that you said. But the notion that perhaps Congress needs to be evaluating and asking the agencies, what are the things that we have done that impede your ability to do what we need you to do now, that may have made sense back when, but perhaps don't now. I think who knows better than you what Congress can do to get involved and, you know, to create situations that need to be revisited? So, I appreciate that. I appreciate the fact that you are talking about not just one administration, but just sort of the evolution of the issues.

I appreciate, Mr. Mudd, that you said that women may be the answer to this problem. You did say that, right? You were the one that said that we needed to arm women with smart phones and recognize that they are——

Mr. MUDD. Correct.

Mrs. WATSON COLEMAN [continuing]. The mothers and they are the wives and they are the ones that are losing their family members. Perhaps, you know, in a culture that doesn't feel that women have much value other than to be covered and quiet, just the notion that we really could be a very strong force for peace. Because we understand the loss of life in a different way. I appreciated the things that you said.

General, you said something that really struck with me. I believe it was you. It may have been Mr. Jenkins, though. Somebody said, "ISIS is concerned with the activities in the region. ISIS is about creating its state and its influence in the region. But al-Qaeda still has an interest in coming back and hitting us."

So, I guess my question is to what extent—since I think we have been relatively safe—I mean, there have been things—I mean, we have been relatively safe here in the homeland. So, this administration and Congress must be doing some things right.

To what extent is there the continued capacity to know in advance, particularly al-Qaeda, what it is thinking of doing? Because we hear all the time that someone had planned to do something, and that someone's effort had been foiled by the intelligence that we had.

The other question I have—and whoever wants to jump in and answer, just fine with me—what should we be thinking about in terms of ISIS, not in terms of what ISIS is doing in the region, but in terms of the threat to life here on the homeland?

I mean, do we see ISIS evolving into an external view so that now we ought to be concerned about what they are going to try to do here? Or is it going to be sufficiently, you know, busy over there, and then perhaps we need to be prioritizing our resources and our efforts and our concerns in a different way? So, I would appreciate hearing from either perspective on this question.

Mr. JENKINS. Let me go first very, very quickly. We have been successful in thwarting home-grown terrorist plots. That is largely because of our efforts to—in terms of domestic intelligence. This has been very, very effective. With a fair amount of help from the American citizens and the community that have provided tips.

With regard to thwarting plots from abroad, there again, we haven't been 100 percent successful, but that has been the result of probably unprecedented cooperation among the intelligence services and law enforcement organizations in the world that have enabled us to do this. Plus, our own significant effort.

With regard to ISIS as a threat, I did say that ISIS right now is preoccupied with expanding its territory. It has—it cannot survive as a stable nation. This is a plunder-based economy driven by an internal push to take more territory and continued fighting. So, it has to do that.

We are in the process now of bombing it. We may be called upon to increase our air campaign to help the recovery of Tikrit and Mosul from them. At a certain point, ISIS may decide that it faces

46

defeat. The only way it can save itself is to draw us into some kind of a final showdown. The way to do it is to carry out major attacks against us. It has significant resources, both financial, and resources to do it.

Mrs. WATSON COLEMAN [continuing]. I guess for my last sort-of comment, I am concerned that groups that align with certain groups—we have seen where we have had alliances. We have seen those alliances break down, and our alliance becomes our enemy. So, it is difficult for us to decide who we are going to coalesce with in any substantial or sustainable moment, and to fight a particular enemy. Because that situation has changed from time to time. To suggest that all we need to do is find a bunch of people, or a couple of countries that are going to be working with us, and think that that is sustainable I think is just sort of naive.

I thank you very much, and I thank you, Mr. Chairman.

Chairman McCAUL. The Chairman now recognizes Mr. Walker.

Mr. WALKER. Thank you, panel, for being here today. I would also like to thank the family and friends who have been very patient in waiting on this.

The subject of today's hearing is the fight against Islamist extremism at home and abroad. I want to address that a little bit.

I heard earlier from Member Keating that this is really just a bunch of misfits and, see, losers. I just thought about—of those 21 Egyptian Christians who lost their lives. How many of those that were actually doing the beheading would be considered losers and misfits? I don't think that is a precursor for the damage of barbaric activities that one can—that can go into it.

The question I have—or let me set it up this way. A few weeks ago, we had a few moments with Secretary Jeh Johnson. He said this is not theologically-based. My concern and my question regarding that is that he also said the imams and the clerics are very slow to give up some of the individuals that they fear have the potential of being radicalized. Well, then it can't be both. If it is not—if there is not a theological thread that runs through this—and I am speaking as a former minister of 15 years—who have friends and people who have been held captive—in fact, I am even dialoguing right now with Naghmeh Abedini, whose husband is in Iranian prison due to his Christian beliefs.

The problem is this. It either has to have a religious thread to it, or they are just basically criminals. If imams and clerics are slow to give them up, to me, it tells me there is somewhere there is—even if it is extremist, there is a religious thread involved in this.

I believe that General Hayden asked the question, and even answered it. He said, "What unites these factions?" You said, "Islam." Is it fair to say that if Islam is the noun in this process, the action is the hatred that many of these radical Islamic extremists have for our belief system, not just from a political standpoint, but also from a religious base?

I will start with Mr. Hayden, and I would like to follow up with the speaker. Do you feel like that is a very valid part of this?

General HAYDEN. The leadership of the movement—what has made this global has been their interpretation, and many—and I would agree—would say misinterpretation of Islamic scripture.

They claim to take their legitimacy from the Islamic faith. So, I think we need to respect that. I will say again one more time, Congressman, a lot of people join just because they are alienated, and you have got this whole youthful wanting to be part of something bigger than themselves. But it does matter what gang you join. This gang has certain objectives and it legitimates certain kinds of behavior.

Mr. WALKER. Thank you, General.

Speaker.

Mr. GINGRICH. Well, let me start by saying that to the best of my knowledge, the number of Norwegian Lutheran terrorists has been de minimis. To start with that notion—I mean, this whole idiocy that you can't talk honestly about the nature of the people who are trying to kill you strikes me as utterly irrational.

By the way, we had exactly the same experience in the 1940s and early 1950 with the Soviets. You can read Diana West, "American Betrayal." It is breathtaking how hard we worked to hide from the degree of Soviet penetration because it shook our whole system. Well, you are in the same business again.

So—but I want to emphasize a point here that I think will take a while to sink in for the whole National debate. ISIS is a 2-year-old phenomenon. Boko Haram starts around 2001. Al-Qaeda is a little bit earlier. I have no idea what the various lineages are or the various factions in Yemen or—but my point is, there is a worldwide movement. It is explicitly religiously motivated. That doesn't mean that every Muslim is bad. It does mean that there is a strain of Islam which occurs in two forms: A physical Jihad and a cultural Jihad.

The cultural Jihad definition is very simple. They believe that Islamic law is superior to all other law, and that the rest of us ultimately have to basically yield to Islamic law. Those two factions—the physical and the cultural—are clearly at war with the West. Until we can have an honest National debate and discuss that, and then say if this is true, what is our response?

Mr. WALKER. Thank you, Mr. Speaker.

One of the things that offends me is the high-level involvement of human and sex trafficking that these particular factions are involved in, raising the revenue into the hundreds of millions of dollars.

Part of it is this concept—that as a person of a Judeo-Christian faith, there are dozens of places that if you were to enter, you would have loss of life or torture, but there is no place like that where an radical Islamist can enter where he has to be that concerned. So, I want us to look at it from—globally.

The last thing—I will conclude with this since my time is expired—I appreciate your—I think it was your words—this is a willful denial of objective reality. If it is okay, I will tweet that out a little bit later. With that, I yield back. Thank you.

Chairman McCAUL. The Chairman recognizes Mr. Richmond.

Mr. RICHMOND. First of all, let me thank you, Mr. Chairman, for having the hearing. I think this was a very productive hearing. Hearing from people who know what they are talking about.

My sense—and why I ran for Congress and why I am here—is to try to get to the solutions, and ask anybody who has the ability to offer some expertise on trying to figure out an answer. Which means simply, know what you know and know what you don't know. The things you don't know, ask the people who do.

But while we are here, it just reminds me of the circus atmosphere of Congress, and the fact that we don't put on a unified front to our enemies. To the extent that we are continuously—and even here today, the question was: Can you rate the administration's effort against the enemies? As opposed to, can you rate our efforts against the enemies, and what can we do?

Mr. Speaker, you were asked a question about the lack of flexibility. I think someone else—and I think it was Mr. Mudd, who talked about agility for our troops and our strategists and what we can do. You can explain it all day, but you can't understand it for us. My frustration is the fact that I think we are so blind in partisanship that we just won't sit down and listen.

I want to just ask, am I getting the right takeaways? First was the agility and flexibility and find out what we have done as a Congress to limit the hands of our forces, and clearly defining the left and right borders of what we consider acceptable behavior, and not going backwards afterwards with hearings and hearings and hearings, and wasting resources and time.

Also the fact that drones are very, very productive and it causes a certain amount of fear, because it takes away their leadership's ability to have time and safe havens to plot out what they want to do.

The other thing we can do is have hearings and do things as a Congress to figure out the benefits of the targeted killing programs and things of that like to see how effective it was and how it would help us here, and then assert our own thing.

So part of, I guess my question is: Do you think that a focused Congress on the issues that we raised here, with the ability to hold hearings and other things—and Mr. Speaker, you know them better than I, do you think we have the tools to add to this fight? The question was whether it's criminals, thugs, or a thread of religious tone. Well, it is both—it is criminal thugs who are using religion to push their sinister goals, and they are winning the propaganda war on the fact that they have some good mission behind it.

So, Mr. Speaker, do we have the tools to do it? If so, where do we go from here in your opinion?

We can take that question and go down the line.

Mr. GINGRICH. Well, let me just say that the founding fathers were amazingly wise. They created institutions that have enormous capability.

As early as 1793, 1794, they were debating whether or not to complete frigates in order to go and intimidate the Barbary pirates. They decided not to because the negotiations were going pretty well, and had to go back later and finish them.

But the Congress has a long history of being involved in trying to understand, what are our National security interests and what do we need to do about them?

I would say—the point you have made, which several Members have made—if we could get beyond partisanship to have a real National security and homeland security debate, and engage the entire Congress as General Hayden said, in creating a consensus that could last—the Cold War consensus lasted over 40 years, because people argued it out, thought it through, and decided, you know, it is what we have to do.

We need a similar dialogue, and it needs to transcend Democrat, Republican, and be an American dialogue.

General HAYDEN. I second that Congressman. When I was director at the CIA, we consciously made a decision not to do some things that frankly were—we believe were legal, maybe even somewhat effective, in order to build the kind of political consensus that the Speaker just described.

In other words, I would even be willing to perhaps not be as bold as I would otherwise be in order not to face an on/off switch every 24 months.

Mr. MUDD. Just one quick comment on this. One of the things I worried about most when I was in the service wasn't just the adversary. It related to American citizens, and that is there have been debates over the past several years about how we look at American citizens, in particular how we look at their digital trail.

I would encourage you again bipartisan to make sure you clearly understand what you have asked particularly the FBI to do with data and what limitations that provides them. Data is moving so fast; how much digital trail each American gives. I was always concerned we are over-collecting; we are under-collecting; we are on the wrong person; we are using the wrong criteria. I know it sounds like a technical issue. It is fundamental to the hunt for unknowns in the United States.

How much latitude do you want to give Federal agencies to chase Americans' data? How can they collect it and how can they analyze it, and make sure you distinguish between the two, fundamental difference. It is okay, in my opinion, if you collect it; I want to know how you are going to use it; very different from an analyst perspective.

Chairman MCCAUL. The gentleman's time has expired.

Mr. RICHMOND. Thank you, Mr. Chairman. I yield back.

Chairman MCCAUL. The Chairman recognizes the ever-patient Ms. McSally.

Ms. MCSALLY. Thank you, Mr. Chairman.

Thank you panel. I really appreciate all your perspectives today. I agree with a lot of what was said today. Some of my perspectives are formed from 26 years in the military. My last assignment, running counter-terrorism operations for AFRICOM and the tremendous frustrations that we experienced as we watched some of these threats that have been going on for decades, but are continuing to grow and metastasize in their capabilities, both al-Shabaab, AQAP across the way, Boko Haram, AQIM and us not declaratively stating that this is in our National interests to address these threats.

They are growing these safe havens. We could have done some things to address them, and now all of a sudden they are—you know, they are rearing their ugly heads, but we have watched it grow, and we have done nothing about it.

So ISIS is the latest, but these extremists organizations have been growing and metastasizing for a long time, so I appreciate everybody's perspectives on that.

Also a tremendous fan of drones. As a person who is a pilot, that sounds funny that I would be supporting unmanned, or un-womanned, aircraft, but I testified before the Senate last year on that.

Look, if we decide that it is legal to use lethal force and we decide it is good policy, that provides us persistence and tremendous oversight to be able to use those assets, so I agree. So thanks for talking about that.

I have a question, sort of the big picture. Speaker Gingrich, I would appreciate your perspectives on this first, is it seems like right now we are doing the second-graders with the soccer ball—we are addressing ISIS. Oh my gosh, we have got to deal with it. We will do whatever it takes to try to and address that, to include tolerating Soleimani leading the effort to also tolerate that it really emboldened Assad, that Iran's, you know, hand is strengthening in the region, and it just seems like we are looking very tactically at this threat instead of strategically.

As we look at strengthening Iran's hand as the largest state sponsor of terror as an unintended consequence, that is very concerning to me in their capabilities march, you know, of militant Islam.

I do agree with Prime Minister Netanyahu, who said, in this case, the enemy of our enemy is our enemy, and not our friend. It seems like people are looking at it like it is a seesaw, like either we are going to deal with ISIS, and therefore we are strengthening Assad and Iran, or the other way around, like it is one or the other.

Is there a strategic framework where we could be addressing both of those threats? Because obviously our Sunni allies in the region are on the sidelines because of this dynamic, and that is part of why they are not participating fully. So how do we strategically address both of those threats? What would we do differently, Speaker Gingrich?

Mr. GINGRICH. Well, first of all we are missing two key ingredients that we had in the late 1940s. George Kennan wrote what was called ''the long telegram'' in 1946 which explained that the Soviet Union was a world-wide competitor and that we had to collide with it and had no choice.

That changed Washington's view dramatically. In 1950, NSC finished writing NSC–68 which really set the framework for the entire Cold War and was a very long-range document.

So I would say we currently don't have either of those, and that—I want to say, I think this has been a bipartisan problem. I think that what happened is we got sucked into tactical decisions and at best operational decisions, we had very little strategic thinking and very little strategic decision making for a very human reason.

If you really look at this—and I had this experience, I was at the agency in December 2001. The counterterrorism guys were giving me a briefing. They said—I said, what is your target set? They said, about 5,000 people.

I said, what is the recruiting base? They said, oh, 3 to 5 percent of Islam. So I said, wait a second, that is 39 million to 65 million people. They nodded at me. They said, yes, that is right.

I said—and they said, we can't get the White House to understand this isn't about 5,000 people. So I took one page. I had a really big circle that had 39–65 million, and then a really tiny circle that said 5,000.

I went and I saw Rice and Cheney and Rumsfeld, and I said, this is the moment in "Jaws" where the police chief says "we need a bigger boat."

Now the fact is the boat we need is so big, and it has taken us a decade more to begin to realize it, this ain't going away. This is going to get worse. Now I think we are on the edge of being able to have a genuine bipartisan debate that really transcends just fighting over the President, and gets into the question, given that this is true, what do we need to do about it?

Until we have that debate, and understand, Iran is our mortal enemy.

Ms. McSALLY. Right.

Mr. GINGRICH. Radical Sunni behavior is our mortal enemy. These are not marginal enemies. These are mortal enemies comparable to Nazi Germany and the Soviet Union.

Until we are prepared to deal with them at that level and understand that it is a world-wide epidemiology problem, particularly on the Sunni side, and it is a very specific state problem on the Iranian side, people don't want to think like that because it leads you to make decisions that are too frightening.

Ms. McSALLY. Great. Thanks.

General Hayden, any insights?

General HAYDEN. Yes. Congresswoman, your story about chasing the rabbit in Africom brings a thought to mind. You have got these franchises popping up. I always pictured them to be very difficult decisions.

Like let's take Boko Haram, all right? It doesn't appear to be an enemy of the United States. They are not killing our people. They are not threatening to kill our people. Do I really want to put an American face on suppressing Boko Haram and thereby accelerate or even create something that would not have existed in terms of a threat?

The longer I look at this, though, the more I see the connective tissue between these different groups. This is more in the form of a question. I have not yet arrived at an answer.

But if it is right that the connective tissue is stronger than we have seen, that they are part of a globalized movement that the Speaker has described, that changes your—the character of your decision making over here as to how quickly you want to put an American face on going after some of these movements.

Ms. McSALLY. Exactly. Great. Thank you.

My time has expired, I appreciate it. I yield back. Thank you, Mr. Chairman.

Chairman McCAUL. Thank you.

Let me thank the witnesses. I just want to close with, you know, my father was a bombardier on a B–17 in the European theater. They were all-in to win. We defeated fascism.

The long-term struggle against communism that, Mr. Speaker, as you mentioned, we had a plan laid out and a strategy to defeat communism. We won.

Now we face Islamist extremism. It will be a long-term ideological struggle. But I do think in the end we win this one as well.

I also finally want to thank the Speaker who had something to do with this hearing. I read his opinion piece and was inspired to put this hearing together because I think it is important that Congress has a role, an oversight role, and a role to have hearings to draw attention to the American people on this issue and shape the policies that impact the security of the United States.

So let me thank you for that as well.

With that, this hearing stands adjourned.

[Whereupon, at 1:01 p.m., the committee was adjourned.]